# SPIRITED WOMEN

# SPIRITED WOMEN

MAKERS, SHAKERS, and TRAILBLAZERS
in the WORLD of COCKTAILS

SAMMI KATZ & OLIVIA McGIFF

UNION
SQUARE
& CO.

NEW YORK

ISBN 978-1-4549-4446-1
ISBN 978-1-4549-4447-8 (e-book)

For information about custom editions, special sales, and premium purchases,
please contact specialsales@unionsquareandco.com.

Printed in China

2 4 6 8 10 9 7 5 3 1

unionsquareandco.com

Editor: Caitlin Leffel
Designer: Olivia McGiff
Art Director: Lisa Forde
Project Editor: Ivy McFadden
Production Manager: Terence Campo

World Map . . . . . . . . . . . . . . . . . . . . . . . . . . . 6

Introduction . . . . . . . . . . . . . . . . . . . . . . . . . 8

Cocktail Basics . . . . . . . . . . . . . . . . . . . . . . 12

Makers . . . . . . . . . . . . . . . . . . . . . . . . . . . . . 16

Lesley Gracie
Victoria Eady Butler
Morgan McLachlan
Claire Marin
Bertha González Nieves
Karen Hoskin
Stephanie Macleod
Selena Nishihira

Carlie Dyer
Dr. Anne Brock
Andrea Wilson
Carmen Villarreal & Rocío
    Rodriguez
Nicole Austin
Jill Kuehler & Molly Troupe
Dr. Joy Spence

Shakers . . . . . . . . . . . . . . . . . . . . . . . . . . . . . 84

Tiffanie Barriere
Mariah Kunkel
Julia Momosé
Marva & Myriam Babel
Lynnette Marrero
Shannon Mustipher
Renauda Riddle & Angela
    Barnes

Kelsey Ramage
Misty Kalkofen
Talia Baiocchi
LP O'Brien
Chockie Tom
Jenny Nguyen

Trailblazers . . . . . . . . . . . . . . . . . . . . . . . . . 138

Aubrey Slater
Louise McGuane
Carolyn Kim
Mallory O'Meara
Jacine Rutasikwa
Yola Jimenez
Lauren Chitwood, Abbey
    Ferguson & Lexie Larsen
Romina Scheufele
Lola Pedro

Alexandra Dorda
Jess Kandalaft
The Nonino Women
Nitzan Podoswa Marrun
Stephanie Jordan
Effie Panagopoulos
Bridgette Taylor
Eileen Wayner, Alex Smith
    & Lola Thomas

Additional Recipes . . . . . . . . . . . . . . . . . . . 216

Acknowledgments . . . . . . . . . . . . . . . . . . . 219

Spirits Index . . . . . . . . . . . . . . . . . . . . . . . . 220

Index . . . . . . . . . . . . . . . . . . . . . . . . . . . . . . 222

CONTENTS

When I joined the team of a popular Manhattan cocktail bar in 2015, I was ecstatic. It was at the start of my bartending journey. I didn't know then that I would eventually dedicate my whole career to spirits and cocktails, but I was so excited to be welcomed into this elite group of cocktail bartenders. During my second shift, I learned that not only was I the lone female bartender on staff, but I was also the *very first* female bartender. The bar had already been open for five years. When I asked the (male) managers why this was the case, I got a variety of responses like, "it just happened that way," or "not a lot of qualified women applied," or "it wasn't intentional, we just hired the best people for the job." Don't get me wrong, I loved working at that bar. Every one of my coworkers was amazing, and I consider my time there as foundational to my career. But yeah, I dealt with my fair share of sexism. I was once asked by a male guest why I wore a vest and tie like the guys instead of a skimpy black dress like the servers, all of whom were, of course, women. Just the fact that the uniform for bartenders was a vest and tie says it all! Me being behind that bar shaking up cocktails was a radical thing, even in 2015.

Not that many decades earlier, there was *Goesaert v. Cleary*, a 1948 Supreme Court ruling that upheld a Michigan law prohibiting women from tending bar unless her father or husband owned the establishment. Other similar laws popped up around the country, laws that banned women not only from tending bar, but from sitting at bars or even setting foot in them. This decision was overruled in 1976, but

it was only two years prior that a woman could even open her own bar tab without a man's approval, when the ratification of the Equal Credit Opportunity Act meant a single woman could get a credit card in her own name. By that time, the Beatles had already broken up. There was already a *second* remake of *A Star Is Born*. Man had walked on the moon, and Woman couldn't open a freakin' bar tab.

Humans have been consuming alcohol basically since the dawn of time. Women have been drinking alcohol since it was invented, but they've also been making it and serving it since then, too. There were women who brewed beer in the Middle Ages, women who ran dramshops throughout London's gin craze, female bootleggers who made a killing during Prohibition. Women have been involved in every part of the alcohol industry going back to ancient civilization. In fact, a woman named Maria Hebrea (also known as Mary the Jewess) invented the first piece of distilling technology, all the way back in 100 CE!

And yet, the world of spirits and alcohol is still thought of as masculine. Men drink serious liquor, like whiskey, while women drink cosmos. Men are bartenders, women are cocktail servers. There are real, historical reasons as to why these stereotypes came to be, and some people still believe these worn-out clichés. The purpose of this book is to help debunk those entrenched,

INTRODUCTION

misogynist ideas by celebrating women who have spent their careers shattering these outdated notions, women who have made delicious contributions to the drink space, women who pulled up a stool at the bar and made room for others to feel welcome.

Olivia and I are cocktail people, through and through. We love drinking cocktails, we love making cocktails, and we believe that cocktails are a vehicle for telling stories. Every woman in this book has a story worth sharing. This is not a history book, but rather a collection of profiles of modern-day women currently working in spirits, with each profile accompanied by an original cocktail recipe. The more stories we hear about women kicking ass in this industry, the more customary it will be to hear about female bar owners, bartenders, distillers, blenders, founders of liquor brands, CEOs of major alcohol companies. Hopefully soon, we won't have to put the qualifier of "woman" or "female" before any job description. But in the grand scheme of things, it is still revolutionary to be a woman in spirits.

For this book, we spoke with fifty-five women around the world, operating in all different facets of the industry. We worked to diversify the group of women over a broad range of job titles, spirit categories, and geographic locations. There's a master distiller of shochu in Japan; a founder of a witchcraft-inspired vodka brand in New York; owners of a queer bar in Chicago; generations of women making grappa in Italy; an entrepreneur reclaiming a regional Nigerian spirit and bringing it to the global stage. We wanted to showcase women across every aspect of this business, whom we separated into three categories: Makers, women who are directly involved with making the liquid itself; Shakers, women who are doing their part to shake up the industry, primarily through cocktails or in bars; and Trailblazers, women who have founded their own companies or otherwise are creating new spaces in the world of spirits. Each profile is paired with an original cocktail recipe that echoes the woman's story and showcases their spirit, in every sense of the word.

Of course, sexism isn't just a thing of the past. Women continue to face discrimination in the spirits business (and every business, for that matter). Some women chose to talk to us about their fight against sexism; others didn't, or felt they hadn't dealt with hardships due to gender. Yet, when speaking with each person, we specifically did not ask, "what is it like to be a woman in this industry?" Answering that question is exhausting, and frankly, there are more compelling questions to ask, like "what communities have uplifted you and your work?" or "what have been some of the biggest challenges in your career?" or "what excites you most about the future of the spirits industry?"

A project of this scale wasn't without its difficulties. Olivia and I are based in New York and had to conduct most of our interviews via Zoom or over the phone. We were limited to highlighting spirits that are available in the American market, as most of our readers are in the United States. We (sadly) are only fluent in English, so we had to find people who either spoke the same language or had access to a translator. We also only had about a year and a half to do all of this.

But even with these limitations, it was a challenge to narrow down the list. It was an embarrassment of riches! With each interview we conducted, we learned about other amazing women doing astounding work in this industry. There are so many women triumphing in this business today that we couldn't possibly include them all. And we just stuck to spirits! This doesn't include any of the badass ladies working in beer, wine, or other arenas in the beverage space.

The women you'll meet in this book are distillers, blenders, spirits experts, bartenders, founders, owners of small businesses, leaders of large companies. They are authors, educators, mothers, humanitarians, executives, advocates, historians, musicians, directors, designers, storytellers. They are thoughtful, inquisitive, courageous, kind, funny, brilliant, generous, hardworking. We hope you are inspired by their stories, make a few cocktails, and raise your glass in honor of these incredible Spirited Women.

Before we meet all these amazing women, here are some cocktail fundamentals you'll need to know in order to make the drinks in this book.

# Spirits

**VODKA:** A neutral grain spirit that can be made from any fermentable plant or fruit, but most commonly wheat, potatoes, or corn.

**GIN:** A neutral grain spirit distilled with juniper and other botanicals. Typically piney and citrusy, gin varies in flavor based on what botanicals were used in the distillation.

**RUM:** A spirit made from sugarcane or its by-products. It can be aged or unaged, and made anywhere in the world in a wide variety of styles, so it's an enormously diverse spirit category.

**AGAVE:** Tequila and mezcal are made from the agave plant, and as a category are collectively known as agave spirits. Both must be made in Mexico; they can be aged or unaged, in categories called blanco (unaged), reposado (aged two to twelve months), and añejo (aged one to three years).

**WHISK(E)Y:** Another broad spirit category. All whiskeys are distilled from grain and aged in barrels. The most common types are **bourbon whiskey**, which is made in America from at least 51 percent corn and tends to be sweet; **rye whiskey**, which is made from at least 51 percent rye grain and tends to be spicy; and **Scotch whisky**, which is made in Scotland and tends to be smoky.

**BRANDY:** A spirit distilled from fermented fruit juice, most commonly grapes or apples. It can be aged or unaged. There are many different types and styles of brandy.

**ABSINTHE:** An overproof spirit that tastes of wormwood and anise. It's usually used sparingly in cocktails because it's pretty intense, both in flavor and in alcohol content.

**FORTIFIED WINES:** These are wines that have distilled spirits added to them to increase their alcohol content and shelf life. **Vermouth** is the most well-known fortified wine, and is fortified with a neutral spirit, then flavored with herbs and spices. The most common categories are dry vermouth, sweet vermouth, and blanc vermouth. **Sherry** is made in the Jerez region of Spain and comes in dry styles (such as fino), semidry styles (such as amontillado), and sweet styles (such as Pedro Ximénez). Always store fortified wines in the fridge once they've been opened!

**LIQUEURS:** These are essentially distilled spirits with added flavorings and sweeteners. A few important ones are **triple sec** (orange liqueur; one of the most popular brands is Cointreau), **Campari** (bitter orange), **Chartreuse** (herbal liqueur that comes in both green and yellow varieties), and **St-Germain** (elderflower liqueur).

**AMARI:** The plural of amaro, these are bittersweet liqueurs made of herbs, roots, and spices that come mainly from Italy but can be produced anywhere in the world.

**BITTERS:** High-proof spirits with added herbs, barks, spices, and roots used as a flavoring agent in cocktails, usually measured in dashes or drops. The most common bitters are **Angostura bitters** (a secret recipe with a distinct, herbal flavor), **orange bitters**, and **Peychaud's bitters** (tastes of anise and cherry).

**NONALCOHOLIC INGREDIENTS:** Also very important when making cocktails are **juices**. Please squeeze your own citrus! Lemons, limes, grapefruits—fresh juice will be so much better than the bottled stuff, I promise. With other juices like pineapple or pomegranate, feel free to use store-bought. **Sweeteners**, such as simple syrup, should also be homemade (see page 218). **Seltzer** is good to have on hand, as is **tonic water**. Always have plenty of **ice** in your freezer, both smaller cubes and big ice cubes (you can buy silicone molds for these). For crushed ice, just break up some small cubes into even smaller pieces.

# TOOLS

**SHAKER TINS:** A two-piece set made up of one larger tin and one smaller tin.

**STRAINERS:** A Hawthorne or coil strainer, for shaken drinks. A julep strainer, for stirred drinks. A fine strainer, for double straining drinks.

**MIXING GLASS:** Any glass vessel that can hold liquid and ice, ideally with a spout.

**JIGGER:** A measuring device that has 2-ounce, 1-ounce, ¾-ounce, ½-ounce, and ¼-ounce markings.

**BARSPOON:** A long-handled spoon used to stir cocktails.

**MUDDLER:** Used to break up any solid ingredients, like fruits, herbs, or sugar cubes.

**JUICER:** Handheld juicer or citrus press. Make sure to strain out all the seeds and pulp before using the juice.

**Y-PEELER:** For making citrus twists for garnish.

# TECHNIQUES

**SHAKING:** Add your ingredients to one of your shaker tins, then fill it with ice. Place the other tin on top to close, then shake vigorously for 10 to 20 seconds. Whack the side of the tin near the seal to release.

**DRY SHAKING:** Shake your cocktail without ice first, then add ice and shake vigorously. Used primarily for drinks containing egg white to add frothiness.

**STIRRING:** Add your ingredients to the mixing glass, then fill with ice. Gently stir the ice and ingredients in the glass for 20 to 30 seconds.

**MUDDLING:** Press down firmly on harder ingredients, like sugar cubes, to adequately break them up. Press down gently on herbs to release their oils (this also avoids making them unpleasantly bitter).

**DOUBLE-STRAINING:** Used to smooth out your cocktail and rid it of any ice chips or bits of muddled fruit. With your non-pouring hand, hold the fine strainer over your glass, then pour the cocktail through the strainer into the glass.

**RINSING:** Used to impart the taste and smell of an intensely aromatic ingredient (such as absinthe) without overpowering the cocktail. Add a small amount of the ingredient to the glass, rotate the glass to coat the inside with the ingredient, then dump it out.

**RIMMING A GLASS:** Place a granulated ingredient (such as salt or sugar) on a small plate. Wet the rim of the glass with water or a citrus wedge, then gently roll the rim in the granulated ingredient to coat. This must be done before straining your cocktail into the glass.

**MAKING AND EXPRESSING A CITRUS TWIST:** Use a Y-peeler to get a swath of citrus peel, without slicing into the pith or fruit. Express the oils by holding the peel, pith-side facing you, and squeezing it over the top of your glass.

The history of women distilling alcohol may not be very well-known, but women have had a hand in making spirits every step of the way. The alembic still was invented by a woman in ancient Alexandria. A woman was responsible for first adding hops to beer in the early Middle Ages. The Champagne industry was revolutionized by a woman in the nineteenth century, and in the same era, women in Ireland and Scotland helped build some of the most successful whiskey distilleries of their time.

When alcohol distillation first caught on in the fifteenth and sixteenth centuries, women were responsible for making the bulk of distilled spirits across the world. (They weren't always respected for it, as you might've guessed. In the sixteenth and seventeenth centuries, somewhere between fifty thousand and eighty thousand female distillers were charged with witchcraft and burned at the stake.) Yet ever since the Industrial Revolution, when distilling moved out of the home and into the factory, the business of making alcohol has been considered "men's work."

Today, the world of distilling is still dominated by men. There's not a lot of data on the subject, but as of 2022, only 8 percent of distilleries in America were owned and operated by women. That figure dwindles to a mere 1 percent when looking at it on a global level. It's a small but mighty contingent, and women are finally taking back their rightful place at the helm of the craft spirits world. So let's toast to these women who are carrying on the legacy of all the female spirit makers before them, and pour their hard work into our glasses.

# MAKERS

# MASTER DISTILLER AT HENDRICK'S GIN

## LESLEY GRACIE

Some say that the launch of Hendrick's Gin in the late 1990s was the start of the gin revival, or the "ginaissance," if you will. What few people know is that it's all thanks to a woman named Lesley Gracie. But Lesley didn't set out to create one of the most iconic gin brands in the world. "I never thought I wanted to be a distiller. It was just something that happened. It's good fun."

Originally from Yorkshire, England, and a chemist by trade, Lesley first started in flavor development at a pharmaceutical company, working to make medicinal drugs more palatable. "Some of the new things we were developing were really quite horrible," she says, so in 1988 she and her husband moved to Scotland and she joined the technical team at the William Grant & Sons distillery. In the late nineties, the former president of William Grant, Charles Grant Gordon, tapped Lesley to create a new gin. "Gin wasn't popular then, so it was a big surprise to us," she says. "Charles wanted something with depth and complexity, something really different to what was available in the gin market at the time." It was up to Lesley to create the gin, but her boss had a few guidelines: He wanted to use two antiquated kinds of stills, it had to contain cucumber and rose, and it was to be named after the Grant family gardener, Hendrick. "Gin still had quite English connotations to it, and what is more English than rose gardens and cucumber sandwiches?" says Lesley.

The use of the two special stills provides two totally different distillates, which helps give Hendrick's some of its uniqueness. One of the stills is a Bennett copper pot still, built in 1860. Charles Gordon bought it at auction in 1966, but really, it belongs to Lesley. "I say to everybody that when I retire, 'I'm taking that one with me, she's mine,'" she says. "So I reckon that when it does disappear, it's not theft, is it?" The other still is a Carter-Head, built in 1948. "Unfortunately, it's too big for my garage, so I'm gonna have to leave her here."

It's not surprising that Lesley ended up creating one of the most floral gins on the market, as she's always had an affinity for flowers and gardening. When she was growing up, she had her own section in her family's garden and would conduct experiments with her plants. "I would pull flowers off different plants and supposedly make my mom some perfume," she recalls. In adulthood, Lesley upgraded to a large garden and filled a room in her home entirely with plants. "It's actually a bit more of a greenhouse rather than a front room, because I've got about sixty-four orchids in there."

When thinking about new products, smell is the most important element to Lesley. "You smell something and it brings back memories," she says. "As soon as I smell lavender, I'm immediately back in my nana's house." A lot of her time is spent in the Hendrick's lab, but Lesley gets inspiration from sitting in her garden and going on long walks with her golden retriever, Jock. "He loves the countryside, he loves the beach, so you get all sorts of different environments just by walking the dog." Walks with Jock have inspired different expressions of Hendrick's, such as the Neptunia, which captures the essence of the sea, and the Flora Adora, influenced by the wildflower meadows of the Scottish countryside.

For Lesley, gin is the perfect vehicle to showcase different botanicals. "I like gin because you can go in so many flavor directions," she says. "You can do herbal, citrus, fruity, floral. Your possibilities are endless."

# A WALK WITH JOCK

Lesley's ideal cocktail is when "you get the herbal and floral together." I wanted to honor that and create a drink that evokes sitting in Lesley's garden. Taking inspiration from a Bee's Knees (a classic cocktail of gin, lemon, and honey), I added both thyme and lavender to the honey in order to make it herbaceous and even more aromatic and to pay homage to Lesley's nana. Elderflower happens to be one of Lesley's favorite flavors, so I upped the florality even more by adding St-Germain, a quintessential elderflower liqueur that blends perfectly with the cucumber and rose notes in Hendrick's. Hopefully Lesley (and Jock) will approve.

Makes 1 drink

2 ounces Hendrick's Gin

¾ ounce fresh lemon juice

¾ ounce Lavender-Thyme-Honey Syrup (recipe follows)

½ ounce St-Germain elderflower liqueur

1 dried lavender sprig, for garnish

Combine the gin, lemon juice, syrup, and St-Germain in a shaker tin filled with ice. Shake until chilled, then double strain into a coupe. Garnish with the lavender sprig and serve.

## LAVENDER-THYME-HONEY SYRUP
Makes about ⅔ cup

½ cup honey

2 tablespoons dried lavender buds

1 tablespoon fresh thyme leaves

In a small saucepan, bring ½ cup water to a low boil over medium heat. Add the honey and stir until dissolved. Remove from the heat, then stir in the lavender buds. Let stand for 20 minutes, then fine strain. While the honey syrup is still warm, add the thyme and use a blender or an immersion blender to blend until incorporated. Fine strain through cheesecloth into a nonreactive airtight container and cover. Store in the refrigerator for up to 3 weeks.

VICTORIA EADY BUTLER

**W**hiskey runs through Victoria Eady Butler's veins. She is a fifth-generation descendant of America's first Black master distiller, and almost 165 years later, she followed in her great-great-grandfather's footsteps, becoming the first female African American master blender of a major spirits brand. Victoria is a strong and decisive woman, oozing Southern charm and hospitality without any fluff or pretense. After a decades-long career in law enforcement, Victoria stepped into her boozy birthright with commitment and dedication, almost like taking an oath. "I have fully accepted, acknowledged, and embraced that whiskey is in my blood," she says.

Nathan "Nearest" Green was the godfather of Tennessee whiskey. If you're not familiar with him, you've probably heard of his protégé: Jasper "Jack" Daniel. Nearest and Jack lived and worked on the same farm in the 1850s, where Nearest was enslaved and Jack was a young orphan. The two became friends, and Nearest taught Jack how to distill whiskey. After the Civil War ended, Jack hired Nearest, now a free man, as the inaugural head distiller of Jack Daniel's. What gives Tennessee whiskey its unique sweetness is the use of maple charcoal filtering, known as the Lincoln County process. Nearest perfected this filtering method and taught it to Jack, ultimately making Tennessee whiskey what it is today.

Despite being the brains behind the operation of what would become one of the world's biggest spirits brands, Nearest and his story remained in the shadows. That changed in 2017, when Fawn Weaver brought his legacy to light by founding Nearest Green Distillery in Lynchburg, Tennessee. In just a few short years, Uncle Nearest Premium Whiskey was being sold in all fifty states and over a dozen countries. It became the fastest-growing independent American whiskey brand. Ever.

Fawn wanted to involve Nearest's descendants in her distillery, a lot of whom still lived in Tennessee, includ-

ing Victoria. "I couldn't pass on the opportunity to help be a part of the team to ensure Nearest Green's legacy is cemented in history," Victoria says. As CEO, Fawn also put together an all-female executive team, a first in the whiskey industry. In 2019, Fawn asked Victoria to blend the first batch of Uncle Nearest 1884, named for the last year Nearest put whiskey in a barrel. At the time, Victoria wasn't much of a whiskey *drinker*, let alone a whiskey blender. But when she blended her first batch, she "just seemed to come alive." When Uncle Nearest 1884 hit the market later that year, it immediately started winning awards in spirits competitions and Victoria was soon appointed master blender of Uncle Nearest. Since then, she has been showered with praise for her

work, including being named Master Blender of the Year four times over by *Whisky Magazine*. (She was also the first person of color to be awarded this prestigious title, and the first person ever to win in back-to-back years.) Even though Victoria had never worked in whiskey before joining Uncle Nearest, she obviously had a knack for it.

Victoria always knew she had an innate understanding of flavors and a keen ability for putting them together. She was the resident mixologist in her family and has always enjoyed cooking, learning from her aunts and grandmother. "There were never recipes. It was a pinch of this and a half a teaspoon of that. That's how I learned to cook," she explains. "I apply that same method when I'm blending."

Victoria is Uncle Nearest's only blender, so she personally tastes every batch of whiskey that goes through the distillery. She tastes and blends at barrel-proof, which means she tastes the spirit right from the cask, without adding any water to it. Most blenders don't sample like this, because cask-strength whiskey is *strong*. If a typical bottled whiskey is around 45% ABV, barrel-strength whiskey is usually about 60% ABV. Only a true badass like Victoria could spend her whole workday tasting barrel-proof whiskey.

Victoria is hugely responsible for Uncle Nearest's success, but her relationship with Fawn is the backbone of the company. "In a nutshell, I'm pretty crazy about the gal," says Victoria. "If it had not been for her and the dedication that she puts in, day in and day

out, we wouldn't be where we are." Additionly, Fawn and Victoria have launched several initiatives aimed to involve more people of color in distilling and invest in minority-founded and -owned spirits brands. "We'll continue to grow and support others who are in the spirits industry, who are BIPOC and who are in need of a leg up," Victoria says. "We will continue to be our brother's keeper and fill in the gaps where we can and where we see a need."

It's amazing to think that Nearest Green's story, almost lost to history, has been revived by his great-great-granddaughter, whose signature is on every bottle of his namesake whiskey. It may have taken her until the age of fifty-eight to tap into her whiskey-making destiny, but Victoria has embraced her heritage with full force. "Things happen right when they're supposed to," she says. "I'm just getting started."

# CARRY THE TORCH

Victoria is a woman who knows what she likes, and she enjoys her cocktails in a particular way: "If I'm sitting outside and we have the firepit going and there's good conversation, it's a perfect evening." This drink is a take on a whiskey sour that really highlights Uncle Nearest 1884, Victoria's first whiskey blend and the company's signature expression. Pineapple and cinnamon, two of her favorite cocktail ingredients, play off the whiskey's sweet and spicy notes. Smoking the glass with cinnamon sticks evokes sitting around a campfire and brings toasty aromatics to the cocktail. The final touch is a torched cinnamon stick, reminiscent of the cigar Victoria loves to enjoy alongside Uncle Nearest whiskey. (Did I mention she's a badass?)

Makes 1 drink

2 or 3 small cinnamon sticks, for smoking the glass, plus
    1 large cinnamon stick, for garnish
2 ounces Uncle Nearest 1884 small batch whiskey
½ ounce pineapple juice
½ ounce cinnamon syrup (page 216)
¼ ounce fresh lemon juice

Break up the small cinnamon sticks and arrange them in a little pile on a flameproof surface like a baking sheet. Light the cinnamon sticks with a lighter, match, or butane torch and quickly cover it with a rocks glass. Combine the whiskey, pineapple juice, cinnamon syrup, and lemon juice in a shaker tin. Fill the tin with ice and shake. Remove the smoked rocks glass from the cinnamon stick pile, add a big ice cube, and strain the cocktail into the glass. Carefully light the end of the large cinnamon stick so it gets a little charred. Garnish the cocktail with the charred cinnamon stick and serve.

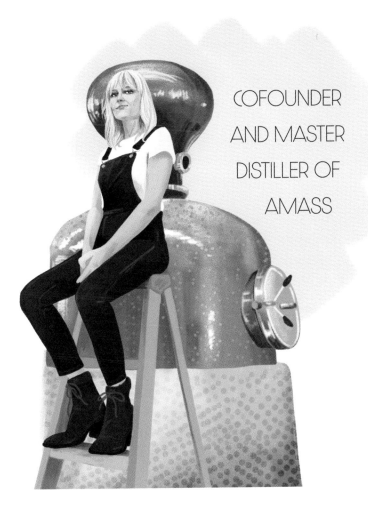

COFOUNDER
AND MASTER
DISTILLER OF
AMASS

MORGAN McLACHLAN

**G**rowing up in the Pacific Northwest, Morgan McLachlan always had a deep connection to nature. She would spend summers on Vancouver Island with her grandparents, playing in the forest and investigating the natural world. "I was very into botany and kitchen-witchcraft kind of things," she says. When she moved to Los Angeles in the late 2000s, she wanted to forge a strong relationship with the native plants and botanicals that grew in her new backyard. "I live in a really interesting little microclimate, and I started thinking, 'What would a regional spirit be made from in Southern California?'" she recalls.

Morgan began experimenting with making spirits from California-grown fruit, as well as "weird, super-wild, witchy gins made with local botanicals." She taught herself how to distill right in her Los Angeles apartment, and from there, she says, "I learned that I really love, love, love botanicals, I love product development, I love distilling." In 2018, Morgan founded AMASS, a spirits company inspired by the California terroir with a focus on domestic botanicals.

Terroir is a French term that encompasses the characteristics of the natural environment in which something is produced—it's a word usually associated with wine and winemaking. But spirits that highlight specific regional flora have their own kind of terroir, and that's exactly what Morgan set out to make. She began working on a gin, the spirit most associated with botany. Most gins are distilled with about a dozen botanicals; AMASS gin is made with a whopping twenty-nine. Some are classic gin botanicals, like juniper and citrus, but most are indigenous to Southern California, like bay leaves (which come from a tree in Morgan's yard), a shrub called cascara sagrada, and lion's mane mushrooms. The resulting gin is flavorful and earthy, and great in both a martini and a gimlet. "We wanted it to be really weird and complex, but I also wanted to make products that are versatile," Morgan says.

Next, she set her sights on vodka. Arguably the most versatile spirit on the planet, vodka is often neutral and odorless, but Morgan wanted to develop a vodka that totally rebuffs the spirit's nondescript reputation.

AMASS vodka is distilled with marigold, lemon peel, and chamomile, which are used both for their aromatics and for texture. The resulting spirit is floral and subtle, but certainly has more personality than your run-of-the-mill vodka.

Morgan also wanted to reflect the elegance of botanicals in more than just booze. While she was pregnant, she was looking for a sophisticated beverage that had nuance and complexity but didn't contain alcohol. "I wanted that sort of sensual drinking experience of having cocktails or a glass of wine," she says. "I wanted options, and I think other people want options, too." So Morgan developed Riverine, a nonalcoholic spirit that pays tribute to her home in the Pacific Northwest. AMASS also started making personal care products from botanicals, like candles, soap, and hand sanitizer.

At its essence, distilling is about transforming natural ingredients into a sensory experience. AMASS's spirits are clearly influenced by nature, and they're also fully representative of Morgan's ethos. "I find botanicals very inspiring, and I wanted to express their aromatic beauty in beverage form," she says. Through AMASS, Morgan is bringing a little bit of the outdoors straight to our indoor bar carts. "Working with plants in this novel way is really fun for me," she says. "And I think we all need and want more nature in our lives."

# EVENING STAR

When Morgan settles down for the night with a drink, she usually goes for a Vesper, a modern martini variation made with gin, vodka, and Lillet apéritif wine. So I riffed on Morgan's go-to cocktail choice, using AMASS vodka as the base spirit. It's accompanied by gin, preferably AMASS, of course; Cocchi Americano, an apéritif wine that's slightly more bitter than Lillet; and génépy, an alpine herbal liqueur whose floral notes play off the chamomile used in the distillation of the vodka. It's an elegant, luscious, and spirit-forward cocktail that celebrates botany. (The name of the cocktail also connects to Morgan's love of nature: Vesper, besides being a tasty martini, is also the Greek name for the evening star, a nickname for the planet Venus when it appears in the sky at or after sunset.)

Makes 1 drink

1 ½ ounces AMASS vodka

½ ounce gin, preferably AMASS

½ ounce Cocchi Americano

½ ounce génépy

4 dashes grapefruit bitters

1 lemon twist, for garnish

Combine the vodka, gin, Cocchi, génépy, and bitters in a mixing glass filled with ice. Stir until chilled, then strain into a Nick and Nora glass. Garnish with the lemon twist and serve.

**CLAIRE MARIN**

n 2003, Claire Marin gave her then-girlfriend, now-wife, Cathy, a beekeeping kit for the holidays. "We set it up and I totally fell in love with bee-keeping," says Claire. "Cathy was like, 'yeah, beekeeping, cool, whatever.' But it literally changed my life." Claire is now the founder and head distiller of Pollinator Spirits, a craft distillery and tasting room in the Catskills, New York, with a line of liquors all made with the nectar of Claire's beloved bees: honey.

Claire never intended to be a distiller. In fact, she worked in magazine publishing in New York City until 2010, when she chose to get off the corporate hamster wheel and spend more time in nature with her bees. She and Cathy made their weekend home in Long Eddy, New York, their permanent residence, and Claire dove veil-first into her apiary. She made her beekeeping hobby into a business by selling her raw wild-flower honey to local restaurants under the name Catskill Provisions.

With the buzz around Catskill Provisions getting louder, Claire wanted to find another way to make a positive impact on the land and her community. "We were under threat of fracking at that time. Every farm in New York was really at risk of losing their land," she explains. Claire discovered that rye is a cover crop, so it helps with erosion, and that New York was once the rye capital of the country. "I thought, wow, what a noble wheat to grow, right?" She reached out to a distillery in the Finger Lakes to make a whiskey using her rye and a touch of honey from her bees. The first bottles of New York Honey Rye Whiskey were released in 2013, and Claire personally went around town selling them store to store.

After four years of working with other distillers, Claire wanted a change. "I said to Cathy, I either get out and I'm super proud of what I did, or we go all in," says Claire. They decided to take the latter route and converted the barn on their property into a distillery; Claire, meanwhile, learned how to distill. Her goal was to create a cocktail-centric line of spirits that were also enjoyable to sip on their own. The not-so-secret ingredient ended up being, what else? Honey. "Honey just balances flavors. When you have acidity or bitterness, honey is your friend," says Claire. "I mean, a little drop of honey is like, perfection." Claire no longer grows her own rye, but she works with local farmers who grow organic, non-GMO heirloom grains. She donates all the spent grains from the

distillation process to farmers in the area, who use it as animal feed. "Giving back to the environment obviously is extremely important because without that, we are nothing," says Claire.

Today, Pollinator Spirits produces a vodka, three gins, three whiskeys, and an amaro, with 3 percent of all proceeds going to pollinator causes. Claire's Crimson Amaro is made from fifteen botanicals, including wormwood, gentian root, sage, and citrus peels. But the secret sauce is adding extract from a tiny bug called a cochineal to achieve the amaro's bright red color without using artificial dyes. (It's not as wacky as it sounds: Cochineal was used to color fabrics as early as the second century BCE and continues to be employed around the world as a dye for fabric, cosmetics, and

food coloring; Campari used cochineal in their essential Italian apéritif before switching to artificial coloring in 2006.) It's another way that Claire harnesses the natural world.

As the queen bee of the Catskills, Claire is affable and generous, bringing her artistic flair to a burgeoning community in western New York. She's a master of channeling the world around us to achieve beautiful products, letting the flavors of the land shine through. But even with the swarm of attention, for Claire, the bees are still the essence of Pollinator Spirits. "The allure for me is being on this planet but in their world," says Claire. "The more you know them, the more you appreciate what they do and how important they are."

# QUEEN BEE

This cocktail is basically a boulevardier meets an old-fashioned in a beehive—it's boozy and slightly bitter, but still approachable, with the unmistakable aroma and taste of honey. The base is Pollinator rye whiskey, which is finished in a honey-coated barrel. The Crimson Amaro (playing the role of Campari) and Bénédictine (a French herbal liqueur with honeyed, floral notes) join forces and balance each other out. And of course, actual honey makes its way in there to tie everything together. The result is a delicious bittersweet cocktail that mellows as it sits. It's classic and sophisticated with a clear vision, just like Claire.

Because Pollinator Spirits are so versatile, this cocktail also works with gin or vodka, in case you're not a whiskey person! And if you think you're someone who doesn't like bitter drinks, this one is subtle enough that you might still enjoy it.

Makes 1 drink

2 ounces Pollinator Spirits New York Honey Rye Whiskey

½ ounce Pollinator Spirits Crimson Amaro

½ ounce Bénédictine

1 barspoon honey syrup (page 216)

3 dashes orange bitters

1 orange twist, for garnish

Combine the rye, amaro, Bénédictine, honey syrup, and bitters in a rocks glass over a big ice cube and stir until chilled. Garnish with the orange twist and serve.

# BERTHA GONZÁLEZ NIEVES

Tequila has always held a special place in Bertha González Nieves's heart. Her first experience with it was at her grandmother's house in her hometown of Mexico City, where the spirit was always on the table. "I saw everybody being so excited to have their glass of tequila," Bertha recalls. "I just wanted to be a part of this beautiful tradition and family ritual."

After getting her master's degree in marketing communications, Bertha headed into the tequila business. She climbed the ranks at one of the world's largest tequila companies, Jose Cuervo, serving as an executive for nearly a decade. In the late 2000s, Bertha left to start her own company, Casa Dragones, and produce her own tequila. "One thing that captivated me is how the world sees Mexico through the eyes of tequila," she says. "Something I enjoy the most is being able to tell the story of the Mexico I grew up in, the Mexico that I admire, the Mexico that has a preeminent role in culture around the world."

Based out of San Miguel de Allende, Bertha founded Casa Dragones with media executive Bob Pittman in 2008. She approached Benjamin Garcia, a tequila distiller she had met during her time at Jose Cuervo, to help craft the spirit. At the time, tequila was still mostly considered a party booze, either taken as a shot with a lick of salt or mixed into a margarita. Bertha wanted to flip the script on the international perception of the spirit, and designed Casa Dragones to be an ultra-premium sipping tequila. "That's the Mexican tradition. We sip," she says. "Sharing that tradition with the world, and convincing global palates that the spirit has that level of quality and sophistication, is something I truly believe in." Bertha and Benjamin decided that if they couldn't expand the tequila repertoire and add something new to the conversation, they weren't going to do it at all. "By trial and error, by being adventurous and trying new blends and new processes, we got to our first product," she says. In late 2009, they released Casa Dragones Joven, a blend of both blanco and extra-aged tequila, something totally novel in the tequila game. It's extremely sippable yet deliciously complex. From there, Casa Dragones developed versions of the

three main tequila styles (blanco, reposado, and añejo) over the course of the next fifteen years.

Environmental sustainability is top of mind for Bertha and Casa Dragones. They hand-harvest the agave plant only when it is fully mature (not always the practice in the fast-growing tequila market), and their production process has been recognized by the Tequila Regulatory Council as the most efficient in the industry. "We have the responsibility to figure out how to build best practices for the future," says Bertha. "What's really important is to make sure that we are pushing the conversation of tequila production so this spirit will have true longevity."

Bertha was named the first official maestra tequilera (female master tequila distiller) by the Academia Mexicana de Catadores de Tequila (Mexican Academy of Tequila Tasters). "There have always been women involved in the production of tequila—they just didn't get the credit," Bertha says. "I think that this should be a representation for younger generations

and in honor of the other generations that didn't get the recognition." What she finds most exciting about her work is sharing her culture and the spirit (in every sense of the word) of Mexico. "I'm a tequila producer in my bones, in my brain, in my heart. That's what I think about every day of the week," says Bertha. "When I see people enjoying our products as much as I enjoy producing them, the connection is magical."

## SOUL OF SAN MIGUEL

For Bertha, I wanted to make a sophisticated, stirred cocktail that honors Casa Dragones's high-end sipping tequila. This is a simple, clean White Negroni variation, something you can savor and enjoy slowly, using only three ingredients. Casa Dragones Blanco is heavenly on its own, but here it's joined by Cocchi Americano, a bitter Italian apéritif, that's been infused with epazote (eh-pah-ZOH-teh), an herb native to Mexico and Central America. Epazote tastes like a cross between mint and basil, with verdant medicinal notes. Rounding out the trio is Salers, a delicate yet earthy French gentian apéritif. The resulting cocktail is slightly herby, subtly bitter, and softly floral, accenting all the notes in the gorgeous tequila.

Makes 1 drink

2 ounces Casa Dragones blanco tequila
¾ ounce Epazote-Infused Cocchi Americano (recipe follows)
½ ounce Salers gentian apéritif

Combine all the ingredients in a rocks glass over a big ice cube. Stir until chilled and serve.

## EPAZOTE-INFUSED COCCHI AMERICANO
### Makes about 1 cup

¼ cup dried epazote
1 cup Cocchi Americano

Combine the epazote and Cocchi in a nonreactive container. Let stand for 30 minutes, then strain through a coffee filter into a nonreactive airtight container and cover. Store in the refrigerator for up to 3 weeks.

FOUNDER OF
MONTANYA
DISTILLERS

**K**aren Hoskin got her first taste of rum in 1988. At nineteen years old, she was living in India when a bartender poured her some regional aged rum. "I fell in love and I thought, 'Wow, what else is out there?'" She spent the next twenty years exploring rum-making countries around the world, including Belize, Jamaica, Barbados, Guatemala, and Nicaragua. "The rum community is full of music and languages," says Karen. "There's just so much vibrancy." It was in the foothills of Colombia where Karen learned about the mountain tradition of making rum. She was so inspired that she brought that tradition all the way back to her home

in the Colorado Rockies. In 2007, she founded Montanya Distillers, a rum distillery and tasting room in Crested Butte, Colorado, and carved out space for other women to follow in her footholds.

The craft spirits movement was just getting started in the late aughts, and the concept of "premium rum" was considered paradoxical. Rum isn't tied to a geographic location, but it's most commonly associated with tropical and island regions, and with her craft rum distillery nestled in the mountains of the American West, Karen was embarking on an unmarked uphill trail. "Rum is still the thing that I find to be underappreciated and yet fully spectacular," she says.

The idea of making rum in snowy Colorado might seem outrageous. (It's not like sugarcane is the state's agricultural cornerstone, and you probably imagine enjoying a hot toddy in a ski lodge, not a mai tai.) But through her expeditions, Karen had discovered that rum has been made in the mountains of Central and South America for hundreds of years. "The environment impacts every single aspect of making the rum, and every impact is positive," she says. Everything from fermentation to the water used in distillation to aging the rums is affected by the Colorado climate, altitude, and location. All the water used in the rum-making process comes from a well and is made from snowmelt and seasonal rains. "By the time it gets to the aquifer, it's like a distiller's dream water," says Karen. The high altitude also affects maturation, since natural temperature fluctuations cause the rum to move more frequently in the barrel, giving it a deep flavor and silky texture.

Karen's impact on the spirits industry has been about more than just rum; she's also spent her career advocating for female leadership in the business. She went to her first industry conference in 2009 and immediately noticed not just the lack of women, but the lack of respect for women. "I would walk in, start a conversation, then a dude would come in and the person I was talking to would totally ghost me," she recalls. "It just raised my hackles so much." Karen started the Women's Distillery Guild (now a faction of Women of the Vine & Spirits) to train more women in distilling and provide resources for the next generation.

Montanya started as one woman's dream and has since grown into a significant American rum brand. In December 2023, Karen decided to take a step back. Rather than selling to a major alcohol company or closing entirely, she wanted to keep the homegrown spirit of Montanya alive. After a year of looking for a buyer and "kissing a few frogs" in the process, she sold the company to two longtime employees, Renee Newton and head distiller Megan Campbell, along with their business partner, Sean Richards.

Passing along the Montanya torch to two female employees truly solidifies Karen's dedication to her craft and her commitment to building the next generation of women in spirits. "They have a lot of big ideas and dreams," Karen says. "I'm so proud to have been a part of that kind of a deal."

# MOUNTAIN CLIMBER

Karen is a self-described "classic daiquiri girl." So I took that drink, put it in the mountains of Colorado, and gave it a bit of an Indian twist to pay homage to the start of Karen's love affair with rum. Montanya Platino, their white rum, is great in shaken drinks, and fresh lime juice is a must in all daiquiris. Fragrant cardamom is the perfect bridge between the smooth rum and the herbaceous pine liqueur. Finally, the cocktail is garnished with a lime coin to represent the Colorado mountaintops. It's just as delectable as your classic daiq, but takes on a global perspective.

Makes 1 drink

1½ ounces Montanya Platino rum

¾ ounce Cardamom Syrup (recipe follows)

¾ ounce fresh lime juice

½ ounce pine liqueur

1 lime coin, for garnish

Combine the rum, cardamom syrup, lime juice, and pine liqueur in a shaker tin filled with ice. Shake until chilled, then double strain into a coupe. Garnish with the lime coin and serve.

# CARDAMOM SYRUP
Makes about 1½ cups

1 cup sugar

¼ cup green cardamom pods

In a small saucepan, combine the cardamom and 1 cup water and bring to a boil over medium heat. Add the sugar and stir until fully dissolved. Reduce the heat to low, cover, and simmer for 15 minutes. Remove from the heat and let cool. Transfer to a nonreactive airtight container and refrigerate for 2 days to infuse. Fine strain the syrup through a mesh strainer or cheesecloth into a clean nonreactive airtight container. Store in the refrigerator for up to 3 weeks.

**STEPHANIE MACLEOD**

When Stephanie Macleod graduated from the University of Strathclyde in Glasgow, Scotland, with a degree in food science, whisky was not on her radar. She first worked in soft drinks, but soon she was invited to return to Strathclyde as part of a whisky research team and became mesmerized by the role of the cask in the aging process. "We put the clear spirit into the cask, and it emerges this beautiful color and flavor," Stephanie says. "That really blew my mind, and I decided that Scotch whisky was the industry I wanted to be in." In 1998, Stephanie got a job in the laboratory at Dewar's, one of the best-known Scotch brands in the world. She became master blender in 2006, making her only the seventh master blender in the history of the company (which was founded in 1846!) and the first woman to hold the position.

As Dewar's master blender, Stephanie creates blends using whiskies from a variety of casks and makes sure the product tastes the same across different batches. She equates blending whisky to putting together a jigsaw puzzle, fitting separate pieces together to make a whole. "People ask me what I do, and I say I basically solve problems," she says. Stephanie tastes each whisky as it ages to determine when it's ready to be bottled, then assigns it to a specific blend. While Dewar's is most famous for their White Label Blended Scotch, she has developed a wide variety of other blends, playing around with cask type and aging processes. And because Dewar's is an international brand, Stephanie has been tasked with creating blends for specific markets. "When I was developing Dewar's 15, I was told it must be able to go with green tea, because that was a trend in China at the time." As a professional whisky-taster, Stephanie is focused on texture just as much as flavor. "Smoothness is really important because I don't think there's a tasting note that exists that doesn't describe texture in some way," she says. Stephanie's deft blending abilities and flavor expertise have catapulted Dewar's to become the most-awarded blended Scotch whisky in the world.

Because Dewar's is a massive company (it's owned by spirits behemoth Bacardi Limited), Stephanie has a team of assistant blenders, most of whom are female. "There are still misconceptions about the whisky industry, and we're trying to bust that," she says. "If women see that it's becoming more of a level playing field, it will encourage them to join us." Stephanie also loves that her team is made up of people from all around the world who can draw on flavors from their home countries and incorporate them into the tasting notes. "I'm just giving one perspective of what I'm used to, so it's good to have that mix of different ideas," she says. Stephanie may talk modestly, but her accomplishments speak volumes. She was named Master Blender of the Year for six consecutive years by the International Whisky Competition, and in 2023 she was promoted to director of blending for Bacardi's entire Scotch whisky portfolio. That's nearly a dozen brands that Stephanie is now in charge of crafting! For a country the size of South Carolina, Scotch whisky is a huge global spirits category, and Stephanie plays a pivotal role in shaping it.

# SILK BLEND

Chocolate is one of Stephanie's favorite ingredients to pair with Scotch, because it has similar textural qualities to delicious whisky: They're both smooth, silky, and supple. This Manhattan-style cocktail pairs Dewar's White Label with chocolate liqueur. Tempus Fugit crème de cacao is far and away the best chocolate liqueur I've tasted—its rich, chocolaty character pairs wonderfully with the vanilla and toffee notes in the Scotch. Punt e Mes, a bittersweet Italian vermouth, ties the two together to make one sinfully smooth sipper. This cocktail evokes Stephanie in a glass: It's soft and comforting, but there's no denying it's a force to be reckoned with.

Makes 1 drink

2 ounces Dewar's White Label Blended Scotch

½ ounce Punt e Mes

½ ounce crème de cacao, preferably Tempus Fugit

3 dashes Peychaud's bitters

Combine all the ingredients in a mixing glass filled with ice and stir until chilled. Strain into a Nick and Nora glass and serve.

MASTER DISTILLER AND CEO OF NISHIHIRA SHUZO

# SELENA NISHIHIRA

The Amami Islands are an archipelago in southwest Japan with beautiful white sand beaches and crystalline blue water. It's the only place in the world that produces kokuto shochu, a specific type of spirit made from a local brown sugar. And it's where Selena Nishihira is continuing her family's rich distilling legacy while putting her own stamp on this special liquor.

Nishihira Shuzo (shuzo means "brewery" or "distillery" in Japanese) was founded on the Amami Islands in 1927 and has been in the Nishihira family for four generations. Initially, Selena never thought she would get involved in the family business; in fact, she moved to Tokyo after high school to pursue a career as a musician. But when her father, Isao, became ill in 2014, Selena returned to the island to assist with the company, helping out wherever she was needed: office work, production, sales. In October 2021, Isao handed over full control of the distillery to Selena, and she became master distiller and CEO. "I saw an opportunity to take the company in a different direction, and I was quite confident in doing that," says Selena.

Shochu is the national spirit of Japan. It's typically distilled from rice, barley, sweet potatoes, or buckwheat, and tends to be around 25% ABV. It's generally light and clean, and is usually served neat or on the rocks. All shochu must be fermented with koji (Aspergillus oryzae, a variety of mold also used in the fermentation of soy sauce, miso, and sake), which gives it

an unctuous flavor. Kokuto shochu is made from koji-fermented white rice and kokuto sugar, the archipelago's native brown sugar. The koji rice, sugar, and mineral-rich waters of Amami combine to make a spirit that tastes of the islands.

Selena has always appreciated shochu's ability to bring people together. "Seeing the reaction on people's faces and hearing their comments, it really hits a string in my heart," she says. When she took over the distillery, she added more freedom and flexibility both to the products and the work environment. "The shochu industry is quite rigid and stuck in a lot of tradition," says Selena. "I just felt that it was time for a change." In honor of this wave of change, she created a new shochu brand called Selephant. "I wanted to produce something that felt casual and relaxing, not so restricted and conservative." Selephant tastes like fresh rice, with a great minerality and

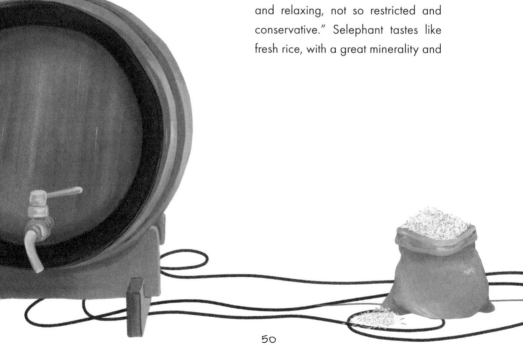

lots of umami. The label looks almost like an album cover—it's modern and artistic, and it certainly stands out amid the other shochu bottles on the shelf.

In addition to running the distillery, Selena is still a professional singer-songwriter. (Selephant is also her artist moniker, a portmanteau of her name and her favorite animal.) Music is at the core of the entire Nishihira family. "Both the distillery and music have always supported our family, financially and emotionally," she says. "Ever since I was born, there's been that relationship and connection." Isao, a former vocalist for a hard rock band, built a music hall in the distillery to link the family's two passions. "With Selephant, I wanted to be able to capture the feeling of our music," says Selena.

One of Selena's new ventures is infusing music into the shochu—literally. The Sonic Aging Project is an experiment in aging distillates while set to music. Each wooden barrel has a custom-made speaker attached to it, and each barrel is tuned in to a different musical genre, including rock, classical, and shima-uta, the traditional folk music of the Amami Islands. The sound waves that are injected into the distillate through the wooden barrel create movement, affecting the maturation process. Selena designed the Sonic Aging Project to be a holistic experience, creating a space for people to enjoy both their shochu and the music.

Since leaving the distillery in Selena's care, Isao is no longer hands-on with the business. "He's quite nervous

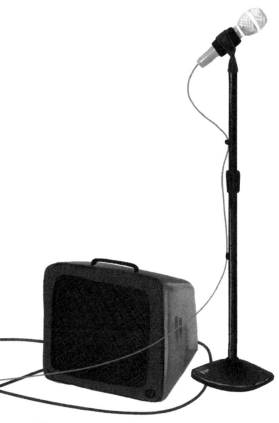

about change and doing all these new things," she says. "I actually told him not to come to the distillery anymore, because I think he might've opposed what we're doing." Selena may have a calm demeanor, but it certainly takes a lot of guts to ban your dad from entering his own distillery.

Selena is both honoring her family's tradition of making shochu and breathing new energy into the spirit. Selephant isn't guided by any industry standard—it's made by Selena's standards. "It might be difficult to change society, but at least within my own company, I'm able to change things," she says. "I don't have to do things in any particular way."

# AQUARIUMAID

For this cocktail, I wanted to highlight the terroir of where Selephant is made, but keep it relaxed and casual to reflect the vibe of Selena's shochu. Quick-infusing the Selephant with nori, a dried Japanese seaweed, both enhances the mineral notes in the shochu and evokes the essence of the ocean. A Japanese plum liqueur called umeshu brings a lovely fruitiness, and the ume plum vinegar plays off this flavor while also packing a punch of salinity. These ingredients are added directly to the glass and topped off with seltzer, keeping the execution of this cocktail easy and breezy. Finally, it's garnished with a lemon twist and an umeboshi in the shape of a bass clef, an ode to the music that resonates throughout Nishihira Shuzo. "Aquariumaid" is also the title of one of Selena's songs, and I highly recommend listening to her album, *message or massage?*, while enjoying this cocktail.

### Makes 1 drink

2 ounces Nori-Infused Selephant Shochu (recipe follows)

¾ ounce umeshu (Japanese plum liqueur)

1 barspoon ume plum vinegar

Seltzer, to top

1 lemon twist, for garnish

1 umeboshi (Japanese pickled plum), for garnish

Combine the shochu, umeshu, and vinegar in a Collins glass filled with ice. Top with seltzer and gently stir. Skewer the lemon twist and umeboshi on a pick in the shape of a bass clef, place the garnish on the glass, and serve.

# NORI-INFUSED SELEPHANT SHOCHU

Makes 1 cup

1 cup Selephant Shochu

1 nori sheet, roughly broken up into small pieces

Combine the shochu and nori in a nonreactive container. Let stand for 30 to 45 minutes, then fine strain through cheesecloth or a coffee filter into a nonreactive airtight container and cover. The shochu will keep indefinitely; no need to refrigerate.

**CARLIE DYER**

**A**ustralia isn't typically in the conversation when it comes to whisky-distilling nations. But in the twenty-first century, the Australian whisky industry is blossoming, and Starward, a distillery in Melbourne that ages their whisky in wine barrels, is arguably the leader of the pack. One of their blenders, Carlie Dyer, a young woman at the forefront of a young industry, is helping to put Australian whisky on the map.

When Carlie was nineteen, her family moved from New Zealand to the Riverina, a large wine region in New South Wales, Australia. She got a job at a vineyard and quickly became so intrigued by the science behind fermentation and wine that she made it her career. After working in wine for a few years, she decided to apply for a job at Starward Whisky in 2018, drawn to the company because of its use of wine barrels for aging. "I did it for fun, just to try something else because I hadn't been in spirits at all before then," she says. At only twenty-five years old, Carlie was first hired as a distiller, and has since progressed into a lead role, responsible for aging and blending all of Starward's single-malt whiskies.

Though Australians have been distilling whisky for centuries, the modern whisky industry down under started in the early 1990s. There aren't as many rules and regulations as there are in more established whisky-making countries, like Scotland. "There's a bit more room for creativity here, and that's what I really love about it," Carlie says. Starward predominantly uses red wine casks for aging, so their whiskies are tannic and fruit-forward. After aging for two years, the whiskies go through their first sensory pass; if they're deemed sufficient, the barrels get earmarked for their potential blends. Coming from a wine background, Carlie had the sensory skills needed to become an excellent whisky blender. "I had great mentors, the winemakers in my life who have taught me so much and shown me what a good wine is and what the faults are," she says. "When there's something that is maybe not quite right, being able to pick those things and know what to do to fix them is a skill of mine."

As in other countries, the whisky industry in Australia is still male-dominated. Often, women are overlooked or not taken seriously because of a prevailing assumption that they don't know anything about the spirit. To combat this misogyny, Carlie is linking up with other female distillers in Australia to get more representation for women in the industry. But even a whisky expert still has to deal with the occasional mansplainer. "When I go to a bar and order a whisky, and some dude comes up to me being like, 'That's a man's drink.' It's so tiring," she says. That guy should really know who he's talking to—since Carlie's been on the team, Starward Whisky has won many, many awards.

Carlie loves the challenge of balancing all the different components of whisky to create one delicious whole. "When you drink a balanced whisky, it's just full of flavor and the finish is drawn out. It's memorable," she says. Starward Whisky honors Melbourne, a city "full of casual brilliance." I'd say that's a pretty good way to describe Carlie, too.

# CASUAL BRILLIANCE

Carlie is a huge fan of the Sazerac, a classic cocktail traditionally made with rye, sugar, bitters, and absinthe. The licorice-y quality of absinthe reminds Carlie of a beloved childhood candy. "In New Zealand, we have these red chewy lollies that are anise flavored, and they were my favorite as a kid," she says. This Sazerac variation is bold and luscious, and goes to town on the anise flavor. Starward Nova whisky has notes of red berries, spice, and chocolate, which pair well with Amaro Nardini, a bittersweet liqueur with loads of licorice flavor. Pedro Ximénez sherry is invited to the party; the rich fortified wine adds depth and is a nod to Carlie's wine background. I doubled down on the absinthe, so you get anise in every sniff and sip. This is a robust, spirit-forward cocktail that allows Carlie to have both her candy and her whisky in one fell swoop.

Makes 1 drink

1 barspoon absinthe, plus more to rinse the glass (see page 15)

1½ ounces Starward Nova whisky

¾ ounce Amaro Nardini

½ ounce Pedro Ximénez sherry

Rinse a rocks glass with absinthe. Combine the 1 barspoon absinthe, whisky, amaro, and sherry in a mixing glass filled with ice. Stir until chilled, then strain into the prepared glass (without ice) and serve.

MASTER DISTILLER AT BOMBAY SAPPHIRE

# DR. ANNE BROCK

**A**nne Brock has a doctorate, but she's not the medical doctor she thought she would grow up to be. "I went to med school when I was eighteen, and within seven months I realized I had made a hideous mistake," she recalls. So she did what a lot of people do when they feel at sea in their career: "I became a bartender. Much to my parents' horror, as you can probably imagine."

After working in hospitality for four years, Anne went back to school to study chemistry, a subject she had always loved. "I still didn't know what I wanted to do with my life, so I went and did a PhD, which is often the reason why people do PhDs," she says. She received her doctorate in organic chemistry from Oxford University in 2012, and a friend suggested she combine her love of spirits and chemistry by going into distilling. From then on, Anne was full speed ahead. She first worked at a small craft gin distillery in London, then, in 2017, she was hired by Bombay Sapphire to be their master distiller. In just five years, Anne had gone from being a newbie in the spirits industry to being responsible for the entire supply of one of the most recognizable gin brands in the world. "It hasn't been a classic master distiller route, but it's certainly one that I've enjoyed," she says.

First launched in 1986, Bombay Sapphire is a quintessential London dry gin. The ten botanicals are vapor-infused (rather than being added directly to the spirit), giving the gin a softer flavor. It's balanced and smooth, distinctly juniper-forward with a strong backbone of citrus. Anne runs the distillery, located in the picturesque countryside of Hampshire, England, and her main priority is to ensure that each bottle of Bombay Sapphire tastes the same as the last. To do that, Anne is focused on sustainability. "Gin comes from natural ingredients. All our botanicals are grown in certain areas of the world. If the climate of those areas changes, it's going to affect the way Bombay tastes." Under Anne's direction, all of Bombay Sapphire's botanicals are now certified sustainable. And while she is intent on advancing Bombay Sapphire's efforts to become more eco-friendly, Anne also wants to tell the truth. "I hate greenwashing," she says. "What I don't want to do is plant some trees somewhere and say we're net zero. We're trying to get to net zero, we're doing our best. We're going to talk about how we get there but we're also going to talk about the mistakes we've made as well."

Anne is passionate about getting her team out of the distillery and into the field—the field of cocktail bars in London, that is. Because of her hospitality background, she has a profound respect for bartenders and their craft. "When it comes to creating new gins, you have to know what's going on in a bartender's mind because bartenders are always about five, seven years ahead of consumer trends." In fact, Anne believes bars and bartenders are so crucial to the development of spirits, she moved from Hampshire to London in order to keep her finger on the pulse.

Anne operates from a place of honesty and integrity, and, maybe most important, she knows how to have a good time. "It's very easy to forget why we're doing what we do and to really enjoy what we do," she says. "At the end of the day, we work in the drinks industry. It's fun. It should be fun."

# HYDE PARK HIGHBALL

When Anne was first bartending in the mid-2000s, she made a lot of gin and tonics, and gained respect for the humble highball. "I realized it was a really fresh, exciting drink that you can personalize to your own taste," she recalls. This cocktail takes the gin-and-tonic vibe and adds the essence of a martini, one of Anne's go-to classic cocktails; it also incorporates sherry, an ingredient she loves. But the secret weapon is the sugar snap pea–infused Bombay Sapphire gin, which brings a crisp, green flavor to the drink. This highball is as sophisticated and fun as Anne herself.

### Makes 1 drink

2 ounces Sugar Snap Pea–Infused Bombay Sapphire Gin
(recipe follows)
½ ounce dry vermouth
½ ounce fino sherry
Tonic water, to top
1 lemon wheel, for garnish

Combine all the ingredients, except for the tonic water and lemon wheel, in an ice-filled Collins glass and stir. Top with the tonic water, garnish with the lemon wheel, and serve.

## SUGAR SNAP PEA–INFUSED BOMBAY SAPPHIRE GIN
### Makes about 1½ cups

1 cup coarsely chopped stemmed sugar snap peas
1½ cups Bombay Sapphire gin

Combine the sugar snap peas and gin in a nonreactive container. Let stand for 1 hour, stirring occasionally. Fine strain into a nonreactive airtight container and cover. Store in the refrigerator for up to 1 month.

MASTER OF MATURATION AND CHIEF OPERATING OFFICER OF MICHTER'S

ANDREA WILSON

**F**ew children grow up knowing they want to go into the alcohol business—it isn't exactly a popular career choice for the kindergarten set. The opposite can be said for Andrea Wilson, who first got interested in spirits while on fishing trips with her grandfather James when she was a young girl. "We would go out on weekends and he would tell us stories about his bootlegging days during Prohibition," she recalls. "I was very enchanted by his life journey as a moonshiner." Andrea grew up in Louisville, Kentucky (the hometown of bourbon whiskey), and distilleries were regular stops on the weekend fishing trips. "It was

fun to see things being made. I think that was a huge influence on why I wanted to be in this industry."

There weren't many opportunities to directly study distilling in the nineties, so Andrea got bachelor's and master's degrees in chemical engineering. She first worked at a global consulting firm, but she always had her line cast, waiting for the spirits industry to bite. After biding her time for several years, opportunity finally struck: Diageo, one of the largest spirits companies in the world, offered her a job. "My grandfather had passed away by that point, but it was just the best moment because I knew he would be so proud." At last, she made it

into her dream industry—hook, line, and sinker.

Andrea worked her way up the ranks and became Diageo's director of distillation and maturation for all of North America. In 2014, after nearly ten years at Diageo, Andrea joined the team at Michter's, where she could focus on her true passion: whiskey. "I love the taste of whiskey, I love the aroma of whiskey, I love how whiskey brings people together," she says.

Fishing requires a lot of patience— and so does making whiskey. Whiskey is aged in oak barrels, usually for several years, and as master of maturation, Andrea oversees the entire aging process. She's fascinated by wood and respects it as a crucial ingredient in quality whiskey. "There's over five hundred species of oak. The law requires the use of a new charred oak container, but it doesn't tell you the type of oak you can use, so you have so many opportunities to change the variables," she explains. "There's over a hundred different compounds you can extract from American white oak alone. I feel like it's an endless abyss of information and knowledge." Andrea is ultimately the one responsible for turning the unaged distillate into whiskey. All of Michter's whiskeys are rich and smooth, highlighting the oak's toasty vanilla and caramel notes. "I love the concept of transformation: taking one thing and transforming it into something else I think is really beautiful," she says. When Andrea was hired at Michter's, it was a start-up distillery—now it's one of the best-known newer whiskey brands in America.

In addition to making delicious whiskey, Andrea has had a great impact on the industry itself. In 2009, she was the first woman ever to serve as chair of the Kentucky Distillers' Association, a group formed in 1880. In 2022, she was inducted into the Kentucky Distillers' Association Bourbon Hall of Fame, the industry's highest honor. And as a member of the Bourbon Women Association, Andrea is focused on fostering a work culture where everyone feels welcome. "Part of my passion is not only building the next generation of people who have a passion for the whiskey business, but also creating opportunities for women where they can realize their full potential," she says.

Andrea's enthusiasm and childlike wonder for whiskey and wood are key factors in her success in the industry. "I love learning the why. Like, why does that happen? What does it act that way? I'm on a quest," she says. "Curiosity is my driver."

# FAMILY TREE

"The Manhattan is my comfort drink," Andrea says. "Drinking a Manhattan is like getting a big hug." This riff on that classic cocktail tastes almost like a boozy, smoky peach iced tea, perfect for a summer fishing trip in the South. Allspice dram brings a gentle baking spice note and plays off the spiciness of the rye. The pièce de résistance of this cocktail is the cherrywood-smoked glass, paying homage to Andrea's love of wood and transforming the drink into something truly special.

Any of Michter's whiskeys would work in this cocktail, but I chose the rye, as its spice cuts through the sweetness of the peach; it also happens to be Andrea's whiskey of choice for Manhattans.

Makes 1 drink

2 ounces Michter's rye

½ ounce sweet vermouth

¼ ounce peach liqueur

¼ ounce allspice dram

Cherrywood chips, for smoking

Combine the rye, vermouth, peach liqueur, and allspice dram in a mixing glass. Arrange the cherrywood chips in a little pile on a flameproof surface like a baking sheet. Using a lighter, match, or butane torch, light the pile of cherrywood chips and quickly cover it with a snifter. Add ice to the mixing glass and stir the cocktail until chilled. Remove the smoked snifter from the cherrywood, then strain the cocktail into the glass and serve.

**C**asa San Matías might be an unfamiliar name, but chances are, you've had one of their spirits. It is one of the oldest, family-run tequila distilleries in Mexico and has been in operation since 1886. The women responsible for the success of Casa San Matías, CEO and owner Carmen Villarreal and master distiller Rocío Rodriguez, are both calm, cool, and collected, but fiercely proud of both their heritage and their products.

When Carmen's husband passed away suddenly in 1997, she was thrust into a career she never expected to have. She took over her late husband's role as CEO, initially thinking it would be a temporary, transitional move. But she found she loved the job. "My passion is people. I invest in the team. I always say that I really work for them," she says. (And she means it—Carmen is genuine and empathetic, always putting others' needs before her own.) By making her position permanent, Carmen became the first female owner and CEO of a tequila brand.

There were very few women at the upper tiers of the tequila industry in the late nineties, so one of Carmen's main focuses as CEO was to offer more opportunities for women. Enter Rocío, who joined Casa San Matías in 2005 in the quality control department and quickly proved herself to be worthy of the title of master distiller. From her very first sip of tequila, Rocío wanted to learn how it was made, enchanted by the process of fermentation and distillation. "Ever since I was little, I wanted to research

**CARMEN VILLARREAL & Rocío Rodriguez**

and understand the whole world of tiny microbes like yeast," says Rocío. Working as a master distiller allows her to use microorganisms to make beautiful products. "It's my life's passion."

Both Carmen and Rocío love how rooted tequila is in their Mexican heritage. "To me, it's a privilege to be able to share our culture through the products that we've made," says Carmen. Together the two women have assembled a vast portfolio of artisanal tequilas to fit a large variety of occasions, whether that's a blanco to put in a casual margarita, or a bottle of añejo to give as a gift. "I have the freedom to experiment," Rocío says. "I'm always trying new things."

Casa San Matías has a lot of female employees, and Carmen feels that perhaps more women have applied *because* she's in charge. When Rocío had her first daughter, Carmen could empathize with being a working mother. "It was natural for me to say, 'Rocío, bring your baby to the lab. We'll cover you when you need to breastfeed,'" says Carmen. "I understand these things." Carmen and Rocío's relationship has been built on trust and mutual respect. It's true symbiosis, where they support one another every step of the way.

These two hardworking women have built Casa San Matías into the successful company it is today, and it wouldn't have been possible without their harmonious teamwork. Carmen's focus on creating sustainable conditions for both employees and the environment has garnered much-deserved recognition, and Rocío's skillful and creative tequilas are in cocktail bars all over the world. So the next time you're at your local watering hole, you may just need to raise your margarita to Carmen and Rocío.

# SINERGIA

*Sinergia* means "synergy" in Spanish, and I think there's no better word to describe Carmen and Rocío's relationship. The two women enjoy their tequila in different ways: Carmen likes to sip her (preferably aged) tequila, while Rocío is a huge cocktail fan and usually reaches for unaged tequilas. So I used both reposado and blanco, infusing the blanco with jalapeños to get the spicy kick that Rocío loves. Pueblo Viejo is Casa San Matías's most widely available (and affordable) brand, used here to create a spicy, fruity, and floral variation on the margarita. Because teamwork is so important to Carmen and Rocío, I've included a scaled-up version of the recipe so you can make it by the pitcher and share the love!

### Makes 1 drink

1 ounce Jalapeño-Infused Pueblo Viejo Blanco Tequila
   (recipe follows)
1 ounce Pueblo Viejo reposado tequila
¾ ounce watermelon juice
¾ ounce hibiscus syrup (page 216)
½ ounce fresh lime juice
1 lime wheel, for garnish

Combine the infused tequila, reposado tequila, watermelon juice, hibiscus syrup, and lime juice in a shaker tin filled with ice. Shake until chilled, then strain into a rocks glass over ice. Garnish with the lime wheel and serve.

## LARGE BATCH VARIATION
### Makes 32 ounces (8 cocktails)

Combine 8 ounces jalapeño-infused blanco tequila, 8 ounces reposado tequila, 6 ounces watermelon juice, 6 ounces hibiscus syrup, and 4 ounces fresh lime juice in a pitcher filled with ice and stir well. Pour into rocks glasses and garnish each with a lime wheel.

## JALAPEÑO-INFUSED PUEBLO VIEJO BLANCO TEQUILA
### Makes about 2 cups

2 large jalapeños, sliced
16 ounces Pueblo Viejo blanco tequila

Combine the jalapeños (seeds and all) and the tequila in a nonreactive container. Let stand for 20 minutes, then fine strain into a nonreactive airtight container and cover. Store in the refrigerator for up to 2 months.

NICOLE AUSTIN

"**M**aking whiskey is as close as I could come to making art when I'm only good at math," says Nicole Austin. As head distiller and general manager of George Dickel Whisky, Nicole has single-handedly reinvented and modernized a historic brand into a prominent player in the world of American whiskey—and she's done so artfully.

In 2018, after working in various aspects of the whiskey industry for several years, Nicole got the offer to become the head distiller of George Dickel, a company firmly grounded in the history of American whiskey-making. Made in Tullahoma, Tennessee, George

Dickel first opened in 1878, but before Nicole came on, it was often considered just a knockoff Jack Daniel's. "There were a lot of people with really entrenched negative perceptions about Tennessee whiskey and Dickel specifically," says Nicole. "I felt like I needed to do something big to start to change that conversation."

That something was a big, bold, bottled-in-bond whiskey. Bottled-in-bond is the most restrictive origin statement within American whiskey. To carry the label, it must be made according to a set of legal regulations, including being aged in a federally bonded warehouse under government supervision. Extreme, yes, but by making such a regulated whiskey, Nicole showed that she wasn't messing around. She wanted to make a point with the bottled-in-bond, proving that George Dickel could create high-quality spirits. "If it won awards and tasted really good, I felt like people would be forced to acknowledge that this distillery specifically was one of the great American heritage whiskey distilleries," she says. Her bottled-in-bond whiskey was named Whisky of the Year by *Whisky Advocate* in 2019. "That was beyond my wildest dreams."

In addition to the bottled-in-bond whiskey, Nicole added an 8-year-old bourbon to the Dickel portfolio, as well as a 17-year-old reserve, a 15-year-old single barrel, and a variety of special releases. As head distiller, she's involved with every facet of production, but her favorite part of the job is blending the whiskey. For the legacy expressions, she approves the final product, but for the whiskeys she's created herself, Nicole is the only one who blends them.

One of Nicole's most prized special releases is the Collaboration Rye, a union between George Dickel and Colorado craft distillery Leopold Bros. The two distilleries teamed up to create a rye whiskey meant to taste like a spirit from pre-Prohibition times. "It's what whiskey tasted like in the creation of American cocktail culture," she says. Nicole is a strong advocate for people to drink their whiskey however they choose. "There is no whiskey of mine that's too precious to make a cocktail with, because if that's how you like to drink it, then that's how you like to drink it."

Nicole is a straight-shooter with a deep love of whiskey in all its glory. "This whiskey-making style is one of the few things that we've created culturally that is uniquely American and a real product of the melting pot," she says. "I feel a lot of pride contributing to that legacy and doing it in a creative way." Nicole is certainly doing her part to not only preserve the tradition of American whiskey, but evolve it as well. It's safe to say she has proven to be good at a lot more than math.

# SODA SHOPPE

If there's anyone who understands how to make something stale feel fresh, it's Nicole. For her cocktail, I wanted to do a similar thing to a well-known but dated libation: the muddled fruit old-fashioned. You know the one—it's got cherries and oranges mashed together with a sugar cube, and it greatly offends cocktail purists. (Guilty as charged.)

Paying homage to Nicole's love of American cocktail history, I made two kinds of syrup that are easy to execute; they just require a little patience (and a smidge of math!). Cherry soda evokes the old-timey soda fountain, a vestige of Americana, and here it becomes a rich, cherry syrup. Next is the orange oleo-saccharum, a traditional technique that uses sugar to extract oils from citrus peels. These two sweeteners perfectly replicate the fruit flavors from the original cocktail, but in a sleek, sophisticated way. They also complement the George Dickel bourbon, with its notes of vanilla, cherry, and orange.

### Makes 1 drink

2 ounces George Dickel bourbon

½ ounce Cherry Soda Syrup (recipe follows)

1 barspoon Orange Oleo-Saccharum (recipe follows)

2 dashes Angostura bitters

Combine all the ingredients in a rocks glass over a big ice cube. Stir until chilled and serve.

## CHERRY SODA SYRUP

### Makes 1 cup

2 cups cherry soda (preferably Dr. Brown's Black Cherry)

In a small saucepan, bring the cherry soda to a boil over medium-high heat. Reduce the heat to maintain a simmer and cook until the soda has reduced by half, about 30 minutes. Store in an airtight container in the refrigerator for up to 3 weeks.

## ORANGE OLEO-SACCHARUM

### Makes a scant ½ cup

1 cup orange peels (from about 6 large oranges)

¾ cup sugar

Combine the orange peels and sugar in a sturdy medium bowl or nonreactive container and muddle well. Let stand for at least 6 hours or up to 24 hours, agitating the mixture once in a while. Strain the oleo-saccharum through a fine-mesh sieve into a nonreactive airtight container, pressing on the orange peels to extract all the oil. Cover and store in the refrigerator for up to 1 month.

FOUNDER AND CEO,
AND MASTER DISTILLER OF
FREELAND
SPIRITS

Jill Kuehler and Molly Troupe come from totally different backgrounds. Jill hails from the agriculture and nonprofit world; Molly is a chemist. But together they run Freeland Spirits, a gin and whiskey distillery and tasting room in Portland, Oregon, that celebrates the terroir of the Pacific Northwest, and the power of women.

Jill first became interested in farming and agriculture while playing in her grandmother's garden, and Meemaw Freeland (who, ironically, was a teetotaler) would eventually inspire Jill to start her own spirits company. One night in 2016, Jill was drinking whiskey with

friends when she shared an idea of starting a distillery that focused on spirits as agricultural products, where the raw materials like grains and botanicals were locally sourced. "My rancher friend was like, 'I'll grow it if you make it,'" says Jill. The seeds Meemaw planted in Jill's brain all those years ago were beginning to take root. "That was the birth of Freeland."

Not too far away, Molly was studying chemistry with the intention of being a forensic anthropologist, but she was yearning for more creativity. "I had this epiphany that what was in my glass was actually chemistry," so she got her master's degree in brewing and distilling in

75

Scotland, moved back to her home state of Oregon, and started working at a small distillery in Bend. At the same time, Jill was on the hunt for a head distiller. She'd heard about "this mythical woman out in Bend," and asked Molly to join the team. At only twenty-seven, Molly became America's youngest female head distiller.

Freeland Spirits was established in 2017 and produces gin and whiskey, all made from ingredients sourced in the Pacific Northwest. What makes their gin special is the use of a cold distillation process. Molly had the unique idea to employ a rotary evaporator (also known as a rotovap), a piece of machinery she'd used in a biochem lab in college, as a tool for cold vacuum distillation (instead of traditional heated distillation in a copper pot still). Five botanicals go through the rotovap: cucumber, rosemary, mint, thyme, and honey. Molly then combines the distillate from the copper pot still (made with fourteen dried botanicals) with the rotovap distillate. Together they become one exquisite gin that tastes like it came from Meemaw's garden. "Spirits are such a beautiful art form," Molly says. "It's a lot of chemistry, but you have to have an artistic flair as well."

One of Meemaw's major life lessons for Jill was that women can do anything. From the jump, Jill was passionate about highlighting women in areas where there aren't many at the forefront, like ranching and distilling. "I think every industry benefits from diversity of all kinds, and this industry is hugely lagging in female representation," Jill says. Molly concurs: "I've had a lot of people question me like, 'Are you sure you can lift fifty pounds?' Yes, actually, I can do that. Every woman I've ever met has been asked that question with that same underlying tone of 'Are you sure?'"

To help fight this discrimination, Molly and Jill started a training program to get more women involved in distilling. In addition, they started the Free Spirits program, celebrating female-identifying, transgender, and gender-nonconforming Oregonians who are doing meaningful work in the community. Since Freeland Spirits opened, there are plenty more female-founded and -run distilleries. But for the bold and inspirational women of Freeland, it's not enough. "We long for the day where women make up at least half of the industry," says Jill. "Until then, we'll keep shouting it from the rooftops."

# MEEMAW'S GARDEN MARTINI

A test of a good gin is a martini, and Freeland gin is certainly up to the task. This cocktail has the energy of a refreshing gimlet using ingredients plucked straight from the garden, but takes the shape of a spirit-forward martini. The gin is paired with both dry and blanc vermouths to bump up its floral and citrus notes. (I like using Lustau Vermut Blanco because its sherry base lends a lovely subtle nuttiness to the drink.) A couple drops of saline solution lift the flavors, and the cucumber and rosemary are stirred with the liquid for a full minute before ice is added to chill and dilute the drink. (It's essentially a mini version of Molly's signature cold distillation process.) To garnish, a mint leaf adds an extra aromatic component and voilà! A martini that is fresh and vibrant, evoking the spirit of Meemaw's garden.

Makes 1 drink

2 ounces Freeland gin

½ ounce blanc vermouth, preferably Lustau Vermut Blanco

½ ounce dry vermouth

3 drops saline solution (page 217)

3 cucumber slices, about ½ inch thick, halved

1 rosemary sprig

1 mint leaf, for garnish

Combine the gin, blanc vermouth, dry vermouth, saline solution, cucumber, and rosemary in a mixing glass. Stir for 1 minute, then add ice and stir until chilled. Double strain into a Nick and Nora glass, garnish with the mint leaf, and serve.

MASTER
BLENDER AT
APPLETON
ESTATE

DR. JOY SPENCE

**D**r. Joy Spence is a living legend. She was the first female master blender in any spirit category in the whole damn world. An award-winning pioneer for the entire spirits industry, she used her creativity, talents, and passion to help change the global perception of rum. Any woman currently working in spirits owes a debt of gratitude to Joy and the legacy of her multidecade career at Appleton Estate.

Joy was born in Kingston, Jamaica, in 1951, and developed a passion for chemistry at thirteen years old. She first went to the University of the West Indies thinking she wanted to become a medical doctor. "Well, when I went

there, I realized I just could not handle trauma," says Joy. "I said, no, no, no, no, this is not for me, let me just continue studying straight chemistry." She graduated with first class honors, then went on to get her master's degree in analytical chemistry from Loughborough University in England. (By the way, her final exam scores are still the highest ever achieved by a Loughborough student. So no to trauma, but yes to genius.) Joy began lecturing in chemistry at a university back home in Kingston, then got a job as a research chemist for Tia Maria, a local coffee liqueur brand. After around three years, Joy became tired of the one-product operation, and on a whim, she sent

her résumé next door to J. Wray & Nephew, a large Jamaican rum company. "In my moments of boredom, I looked across the fence and I would see people looking busy and happy, and I said to myself, 'Hmm, that looks like a happenin' place to work,'" she says. In 1981, she was hired at Appleton Estate, a rum distillery owned by J. Wray & Nephew. They had no job openings at the time, but they were so impressed with Joy and her résumé that they created the position of chief chemist specifically for her.

Situated on the southern coast of Jamaica in the scenic Nassau Valley, Appleton Estate has been in operation since 1749 and is now one of the world's most renowned rum distilleries. Jamaican-style rum is rich and complex, unique in that it's mostly pot-distilled from molasses, which provides some of its characteristic fruity funk. It's hard to believe, but Joy hadn't tasted Jamaican rum before she joined the company. "In that period, people just saw rum as this harsh spirit

that you mix, not recognizing that it has these complex flavors and aromas," she says. It didn't take her very long to fall in love with it.

As Joy worked alongside Owen Tulloch, Appleton's master blender at the time, she learned more about the science and art behind making rum. "I became so fascinated with the fact that there's not just the chemistry side, but the artistic and sensory side of rum blending," Joy says. "I realized I could apply my knowledge and passion for chemistry in this art." Having an impeccable set of sensory skills is arguably the most crucial requirement for a master blender, and Owen quickly detected Joy's olfactory abilities, so he took her under his wing. The two worked side by side for seventeen years, and when Owen retired in 1997, Joy took over as Appleton's master blender. Her first assignment in the position was to create a special rum for the distillery's 250th anniversary. But Joy wasn't intimidated. In fact, she exceeded expectations with her very first rum blend and garnered high praise from the spirits industry.

As master blender, Joy's main job is to select rums from all the different barrels and batches, and choose which to blend together. She then makes sure the components meet the analytical specifications (chemistry!), and of course, that the blend tastes delicious (art!). "I think the most interesting part about the blending process is it gives me an opportunity to apply my creativity so I can do whatever I want with all the various rums that we have available to create these flavor profiles," says Joy. "I'm not put in a corner. I can do whatever I wish."

Under Joy's direction, Appleton Estate blends have become a paragon of what Jamaican rum can be. They have what Joy calls "a sophisticated funk," with notes of vanilla, coffee, cocoa, and nutmeg. She's been responsible for so many bottlings that she can't remember how many there have been, but she does have a few favorites. In 2017, Appleton released their Joy Anniversary Blend, commemorating Joy's thirty-five years with the company and twenty years as master blender. She also cites the 17-year-old Legend as her most difficult blend, and therefore her most rewarding. "I was actually reproducing flavors in the original rum, which is more difficult to do than just blending ad hoc," Joy says modestly. That "original rum" is the spirit that was reportedly used to make the first-ever mai tai back in the 1940s. It took several years, but in 2023, Joy eventually cracked the code. Only 1,500 bottles were released, causing a tsunami of excitement throughout the rum community.

As if all of this weren't enough to

cement her legacy, Joy was part of the fight to get Jamaican rum recognized with its own geographic indication. Having a geographic indication is basically like a place having a trademark on a spirit; it means the product has met certain quality standards, and that it's actually made in that place. Joy was on the committee to determine the rules and requirements for what could legally be called a Jamaican rum. The geographic indication was approved in 2016. "Jamaican rum reflects the spirit and passion of our people," says Joy. "It was just a pride and joy to see that we could all sing from the same hymn sheet, so to speak."

Today, Joy's work goes without saying, but when she first stepped into the position of master blender in the late nineties, not everyone was thrilled. "When I was appointed, a lot of the males in Jamaica didn't think that a woman could become a blender," she recalls. "I didn't let it hamper my progress. I just focused on my craft, my skill set, and my passion, and I knew that my work would be seen." Joy travels the world, educating people about Jamaican rum and witnessing her impact on countless women in the spirits industry. "A number of women have seen me and started to cry, thanking me for opening the doors and giving

them the opportunity," she says. "It has been a very touching journey." Joy is also a philanthropist; she personally supports young women in Jamaica interested in STEM, providing them with educational necessities, like books and laptops, that they otherwise wouldn't be able to afford.

Over her illustrious career, Joy has evolved not only Appleton Estate and Jamaican rum, but the spirits industry itself. She's made history and thrown open the doors for women all over the world. She continues to share her passion for rum and Jamaica with artistry, intelligence, and, yes, with joy.

# JOIE DE VIVRE

Joy truly lives up to her name. She is full of vitality and ardor, whether she's blending rum or tending to her favorite pastime: gardening. She has many orchids and flowering plants in her garden, and likes to enjoy a glass of rum among her fauna. "Sitting in my garden room with my orchids, watching the hummingbirds fly around my head, I would just simply have the eight-year-old neat," she says. Joy is also a cocktail lady with a love of daiquiris, so I used the Appleton Estate eight-year-old in a daiquiri inspired by her flower garden. Hibiscus is commonly used in Caribbean cuisine and has a lovely floral quality that pairs excellently with guava (Joy actually has a few guava trees in her garden). Allspice dram, a liqueur made from Jamaican rum and allspice berries, adds just a touch of warming spice to balance the fruitiness. The garnish, of course, is an orchid. This is a cocktail that certainly celebrates the joy of rum.

Makes 1 drink

1½ ounces Appleton Estate 8-year-old rum

½ ounce guava nectar

½ ounce fresh lemon juice

½ ounce hibiscus syrup (page 216)

1 barspoon allspice dram

1 orchid flower, for garnish

Combine the rum, guava nectar, lemon juice, hibiscus syrup, and allspice dram in a shaker tin with ice. Shake until chilled, then double strain into your most exquisite coupe. Garnish with the orchid and serve.

id you know that the modern bar was invented by women? In eighteenth-century London, women were allowed to operate gin shops, also called dramshops. Men drank at taverns, and women drank at these dramshops—one of the first female-centric public spaces. Because dramshops were often frequented by working women who didn't have time to sit and enjoy a drink (relatable), there were long counters for serving. This setup took off and became what we recognize as a bar today.

But while women created the *literal* bar as we know it, the image of a respectable, knowledgeable bartender somehow became a mustachioed dude in suspenders. How did this happen? All over the world and across time, women were banned from tending bar, owning bars, even drinking in bars. (Since a powerful woman was considered a dangerous one, perhaps men thought that there was nothing more dangerous than a woman in charge of the booze.) And despite the fact that in the twenty-first century, about 60 percent of bartenders are women, tending bar is still considered a man's job. Many female bartenders still have to fight for the same respect and recognition as their male peers.

But hell hath no fury like a woman who's been told she can't do something. The new millennium sparked a craft cocktail renaissance, and with it came badass women seeking to make a name for themselves behind the bar. They paved the way for other women to know there was not only a place for them in the cocktail scene, but that they deserved to be there. Today, there are many remarkable ladies making a difference in the bar space, so let's raise a glass to all the front-facing women in the industry who are doing their part to shake up the biz for the better.

SHAKERS

BARTENDER, SPIRITS EDUCATOR, AND COCKTAIL CONSULTANT

f Tiffanie Barriere hands you a cocktail, you're getting much more than just a drink. An award-winning mixologist and spirits educator, Tiffanie goes by the title "The Drinking Coach," serving up delicious libations with a side of history. Her work focuses on connecting culture with cocktails and using them as a form of storytelling, specifically about the Black influence in hospitality. Tiffanie is a teacher who shares cocktail history with effervescence and delight, and as a queer woman of color, she's always unapologetically herself.

Born in Louisiana and raised in Texas, Tiffanie grew up in a household that loved to have a good time. "As a young person, I was like, 'I cannot wait to get to that age so I can party and laugh like them,'" she says. She tended bar at various chain restaurants, and in 2008, she was offered a bartending position at One Flew South, a new, upscale bar and restaurant in the Hartsfield-Jackson Atlanta International Airport. "I thought it was a whimsical, weird-ass idea, and that sounded like me," says Tiffanie. "One month in and I was like, 'This is it. Bartending is my life, spirits are my life, people are my life.'"

After a year, Tiffanie was appointed One Flew South's beverage director, and under her wing, One Flew South won numerous awards, becoming known as one of the best airport bars in the world. With a winning combination of her flavorful drinks and magnetic presence, Tiffanie attracted tons of regulars—which, at an airport bar, is quite a feat. "There are guests that still hit me up," she says. "It was magic." Tiffanie ventured out on her own in 2016, working alongside brands, teaching cocktail classes, training bar teams, and doing pop-ups. The Drinking Coach was a moniker that started as an inside joke, given to her by a friend. "She said to me, 'You're just like this little coach. You're on their side as they drink and you school 'em,'" recalls Tiffanie. "So I was like, 'Let's LLC this thing!'"

Tiffanie first knew she wanted to use drinks as a way of telling stories when she was participating in cocktail competitions. "I wanted to tell a story that was heartfelt, but I thought, 'How do I bring forward a story about Black history when Black American history is shitty?'" she says. "So I just got bold one time and told the truth."

While preparing her take on a mint julep, Tiffanie spoke about John Dabney, the enslaved Black man believed to be the inventor of the iconic Southern cocktail. "It shook the room up a bit, but I won that competition." Ever since, Tiffanie has been using cocktails to teach people about important (yet forgotten) Black figures in hospitality. "It just heals me. Sharing Black stories feels so good to me," she says. Tiffanie was the drinks consultant on Toni Tipton-Martin's book *Juke Joints, Jazz Clubs, and Juice: Cocktails from Two Centuries of African American Cookbooks*, and was a featured educator on *High on the Hog*, a Netflix series about the African American impact on food culture in the United States.

The Drinking Coach serves as an inspiration for others in the beverage industry, especially other Black and queer bartenders. In 2023, Tiffanie won the Tales of the Cocktail Visionary Award, recognized as a person who has helped make the spirits industry more equitable and inclusive. Tiffanie is a true visionary, and because of her, it's clear skies ahead.

# YELLOW BRICK ROAD

### Created by Tiffanie Barriere

Tiffanie is a colorful lady. This cocktail, developed for the menu at One Flew South, is like sunshine in a cup. "My mission at One Flew South was to captivate an array of people quickly with a tasty cocktail," she says. What's more eye-catching than a bright yellow cocktail? Yellow Chartreuse, an herbal liqueur, is a no-brainer, as its vegetal quality plays off the earthiness of golden beets. St-Germain elderflower liqueur brings in a floral note, while gin's botanicals provide the base of the cocktail. The Yellow Brick Road is refreshing and playful, and promises to bring a smile to your face. "There is no place like home, and often in the airport, that's where we want to be or where we were heading," says Tiffanie.

### Makes 1 drink

3 or 4 thin slices Cooked Golden Beets (recipe follows),
about 1 centimeter thick

1½ ounces London dry gin

½ ounce Yellow Chartreuse

½ ounce St-Germain elderflower liqueur

½ ounce fresh lemon juice

1 mint crown, for garnish

Muddle the beet slices in the bottom of a shaker tin. Add the gin, Chartreuse, St-Germain, and lemon juice and fill the shaker halfway with ice. Shake for 10 seconds. Fill a Nick and Nora glass with crushed ice, then double strain the cocktail into the glass over the ice. Garnish with the mint crown, nestling it into the ice "like a sweet smile," and serve.

## COOKED GOLDEN BEETS

### Makes enough for 6 cocktails

4 golden beets, trimmed and thoroughly washed

Olive oil, for drizzling

Sea salt and freshly ground black pepper

Preheat the oven to 425°F. Place each beet in the center of a sheet of aluminum foil. Drizzle the beets with a little olive oil and season with a pinch each of salt and pepper. Close the foil around the beets and place them on a baking sheet. Bake for 40 to 55 minutes, until the beets are fork-tender (the timing will vary depending on the size of the beets). Remove from the oven and let cool, then use your fingers or a paper towel to peel the beets. Store in a nonreactive airtight container in the refrigerator for up to 4 days.

BRAND
CONSULTANT
AND SPIRITS
EDUCATOR

**B**rand development is important in the spirits industry. After all, a brand is just the identity and story of a company that makes it stand out among its competitors, and Mariah Kunkel is all about identity. She's a talented brand developer and gifted storyteller in the spirits business who knows who she is, and is helping others do the same.

A California native, Mariah is of Indigenous CHamoru (Guahan) and African American descent. While she was figuring out what she wanted to do with her life, she did what a lot of people in the early 2010s did: She started a blog. "It didn't really have a focus," she says. "It was just things I liked to talk about," including cocktails, travel, and fashion. What began as a side project soon led to a career in marketing and brand development. "I love creating worlds and working on visual languages."

In 2014, Mariah met the founders of a start-up gin brand called Brooklyn Gin, and they asked her to be their director of marketing. "I didn't even really like gin when I got hired," recalls Mariah. "I enjoyed being a part of the industry and getting to know the bartenders who were pouring the juice." Mariah soon grew to love gin, and used her position to convince other gin-haters that it wasn't just for tonic. "It was eye-opening for me to come on board a spirit I wasn't really a big fan of and come to love it," she says.

Because she hails from a tequila-drinking family, Mariah knew she wanted to eventually work with an agave spirit brand.

The Pacific Islands

After nearly five years at Brooklyn Gin, Mariah became the brand development manager for Banhez Mezcal. "I wanted to be talking about how agave spirits were made, what's going on in terms of agave spirits in general in Mexico." Part of her job was making frequent trips to Oaxaca, connecting with mezcal producers, and learning about Indigenous Zapotec culture.

Spending time in Oaxaca led Mariah to think more about her own identity as an Indigenous Pacific Islander. Working with spirit brands meant she had to visit many different types of establishments—including tiki bars. Tiki is a genre of tropical cocktail bars created in California in the 1930s, presenting a version of Oceania through the lens of mainland America. Tiki bars are meant to be fun and escapist, but for Pacific Islanders like Mariah, seeing narrow stereotypes of Oceanic culture can feel discordant with the reasons we gather over drinks in the first place. "It made me feel worse and worse to go into places like tiki bars," Mariah says. "It became sort of intolerable." In response, Mariah and bartender Samuel Jimenez, fellow Pacific Islander, cofounded Pasifika Project, an organization for people of Oceanic descent in the hospitality industry. It is a collective designed to build community among Indigenous beverage professionals and provide educational resources. "I'm focused on providing context to the conversation, being a conduit of information from these cultures and historical standpoints through a lens of hospitality," says Mariah. In 2021, Pasifika Project was included in *Imbibe* magazine's

"Imbibe 75," an annual list of people, places, and organizations shaping the future of the beverage industry.

Every day, Mariah continues to dedicate herself to making the hospitality industry better for other people who share her identity. "I've never been one to be like, 'Oh, I won't talk about that,'" she says. "I'm loud. I take up space."

# TREE OF LIFE

Mariah's cocktail of choice is stirred and bitter, and while she's learned to appreciate gin, her go-to spirit is still agave. A lot of ingredients typically associated with tropical cocktails, like pineapple, aren't actually from the Pacific Islands. Coconut, however, is indigenous to Guam, and is so integral to the culture that the CHamoru people often refer to the coconut palm as "the tree of life." Since Mariah loves both coffee and Campari, a coconut-coffee-mezcal Negroni felt like the way to go. Washing mezcal with coconut oil gives the spirit a delicate coconut note that provides a backbone for the other flavors. This cocktail is boozy and bitter, boldly coffee-forward with a soft coconut finish.

Makes 1 drink

1 ½ ounces Coconut-Washed Mezcal (recipe follows)

¾ ounce blanc vermouth

¾ ounce Mr Black cold brew coffee liqueur

1 barspoon Campari

1 orange twist, for garnish

Combine the mezcal, vermouth, coffee liqueur, and Campari in a rocks glass over a big ice cube and stir until chilled. Garnish with the orange twist and serve.

## COCONUT-WASHED MEZCAL
### Makes about 1 ¼ cups

12 ounces mezcal, preferably Banhez Mezcal

½ cup coconut oil, melted

Combine the mezcal and melted coconut oil in a freezer-safe container. Whisk to combine, then let stand at room temperature for 4 hours. Cover and place in the freezer overnight, or for about 12 hours. Lift off the block of solid coconut oil and discard it, then strain the liquid through a fine-mesh strainer or cheesecloth into a nonreactive airtight container and cover. Store in the refrigerator for up to 2 months.

# JULIA MOMOSÉ

**B**orn and raised in Japan, Julia Momosé witnessed the work of Japanese bartenders firsthand. At a bar in Kobe, she was mesmerized by the bartender's attention to every drink, whether it was a rum and coke or an expensive martini. "It's not about, 'Oh, only the high-end spirits get the special ice, or only fancier drinks get this glass,'" she says. "No, every drink for every person should be treated with respect and with care and with love. And that has stuck with me forever." This philosophy combined with Julia's tranquil demeanor would make any patron feel like they were in good hands with her behind the bar.

Julia moved to America for college, worked in bars to help pay for school, and soon became interested in drink creation. She credits tending bar at Willow in Baltimore for cultivating her culinary prowess when it came to cocktails. "A lot of my regulars were chefs, and they would bring me random ingredients and challenge me to make stuff." One of her inventions from that time was the Yaki-Imo Old-Fashioned, inspired by a chef who suggested she salt-roast sweet potatoes before infusing them into Japanese whisky.

Julia's approach to making cocktails has remained flavor-focused, often incorporating ingredients from her heritage. But she also knew she wanted to create spaces in hospitality that were inclusive, even for those who don't drink, such as her parents. So in 2017, Julia wrote a call to action for bartenders to make nonalcoholic drinks just as special as their boozy brethren, as well as to reconsider the name "mocktail." "It was always my hope that my parents could have the full experience," not a second-rate or pretend one—and as she points out, "mock" in English language "isn't necessarily a great or uplifting word." Instead, Julia coined the phrase "spiritfree," influenced by a nonalcoholic beer alternative in Japan called All Free, because "it sounded like a choice."

After running programs at other cocktail bars, Julia set an ambitious goal. "I committed to myself that I would open my own bar before I was thirty." At the end of December 2018, just shy of her thirtieth birthday, Kumiko, her Japanese dining bar, opened for service in Chicago. It has since been on countless lists of best bars in America (and the world!).

The first time Julia's parents visited Kumiko, they were blown away. "They sat at the bar, and I made them all of the spiritfrees. They were drinking one that has umeboshi in it, which is an ingredient they're very familiar with but was something they'd never had in a drink before," she says. "They left saying how proud they were of me, which meant the world."

Soon Julia was able to translate her cocktail ideology into writing. She wrote the James Beard Award–winning book *The Way of the Cocktail: Japanese Traditions, Techniques, and Recipes* in 2021, coauthored with Emma Janzen. And ever a champion

for the community, Julia spearheaded the movement to get a bill passed in Illinois that allowed bars and restaurants to sell cocktails to go during the COVID-19 pandemic.

From her spiritfree advocacy to sharing her Japanese heritage in her exquisite cocktails to helping other bars get through hard times, Julia seeks to make the whole landscape of hospitality better for everyone. "It's not the alcohol in the drink that makes it special or valuable," she says. "It's the care."

# CLOAKED

### Created by Julia Momosé

Stir up this cocktail the next time you want to make a sophisticated yet spiritfree libation. It's got a few specialty ingredients that all work together harmoniously. As the base, Julia uses Three Spirit Livener, a fiery nonalcoholic spirit. "I love how it brings a piquant quality to the drink that mingles and dances with each sip." The sour-sweet verjus rouge, the juice of unripe grapes, and earthy hōjicha, a type of Japanese roasted green tea, meld together "with luscious fruity notes and a warming toasted finish." This is a spiritfree cocktail that is bright and citrusy, with grassy undertones and a lingering spice. It's just as calming and inviting as Julia is herself.

### Makes 1 drink

2 ounces Three Spirit Livener
1 ounce Hōjicha Tea (recipe follows)
½ ounce rich Demerara syrup (page 217)
¼ ounce verjus rouge, preferably Fusion
1 orange twist, for garnish

Chill a cocktail glass in the freezer. Combine the Three Spirit Livener, tea, syrup, and verjus in a mixing glass filled with ice and stir until chilled. Strain into the chilled cocktail glass. Garnish with the orange twist and serve.

# HŌJICHA TEA

### Makes 1 cup

2 tablespoons loose-leaf hōjicha tea (available at specialty tea shops, Japanese markets, or online)

Combine the tea leaves and 1 cup hot water in a heatproof container and steep for 3 minutes. Strain into a nonreactive airtight container and let cool. Cover and store in the refrigerator for up to 1 month.

MARVA & MYRIAM BABEL

**W**hen Marva and Myriam Babel were growing up, they would regularly go with their grandfather to his favorite local watering hole in Bed-Stuy, Brooklyn, and drink Coca-Colas at the bar. "We're eighties kids," they say in unison. "It was just so fun, being in that environment," says Marva. "It was a level of comfort and normalcy for us." As adults living in the rapidly gentrifying neighborhood of Prospect Heights, they wanted to hold on to a vestige of the old New York of their childhood. So in 2015, the sisters opened Ode to Babel, a casual gathering space predominantly for people of color and queer folks in the heart of Brooklyn.

Neither Marva nor Myriam has a background in hospitality. Marva has a master's degree in interior design, and Myriam is in the healthcare industry. The sisters describe themselves as yin and yang, with Marva being the extrovert and Myriam the introvert; Marva is a morning person, Myriam a night owl. But they've always been aligned in their vision of curating a safe space where marginalized people can share their creativity and community. Filled with plants and modern art, Ode to Babel was a spot where the music, cocktails, and good vibes were always flowing. "That familiar setting of authentic Brooklyn, we wanted to make sure that stayed around, keeping the pulse," Myriam says. Word spread and soon, Ode to Babel became integral to the Brooklyn community.

During the COVID-19 pandemic, Marva and Myriam started their own spirits brand, Babel Spirits, due to the supply chain issues in the liquor industry. They both love gin (Marva is a gin-and-tonic drinker; Myriam is a Negroni gal) and wanted to concoct one that wasn't so juniper-forward. Instead, the star of Babel Gin is makrut lime, followed by botanicals like ylang-ylang and jasmine.

After eight successful years, Marva and Myriam were ready to move onto their next chapter. In 2023, they closed Ode to Babel and opened a multiconcept membership club called Babel Loft in an old manufacturing building in Prospect Heights, only two blocks over from their original bar. The main area keeps that beloved living room feel of their previous location, but adds in some modern coworking-space aesthetics. While Ode to Babel was a free-to-enter venue, Babel Loft is a members-only club with an annual fee, loosely modeled after social clubs that were built among minority groups in the city (like their father's social club for his Panamanian community). That, coupled with the popularity of places like Soho House, made it a savvy, albeit risky, business move. But it paid off: The founding of Babel Loft was funded by thirty-five investors, almost all of whom are Black, and over three hundred members joined in the club's first few months.

Marva and Myriam are community builders who carry a spirit of generosity throughout everything they do. Babel may be their last name, but Marva and Myriam had another meaning behind choosing it as their brand moniker. "The ode to Babel is learning the languages, so to speak. It could be coffee, it could be whiskey, it could be music, it could be plants, it could be all those beautiful layers," say Myriam. "Learning to listen and speak the languages is where the harmony is."

# OBEAH WOMAN

Created by Laurel Adams, former beverage manager of Ode to Babel

Tropical drinks are all about having a good time with friends, which is exactly the vibe of Babel Loft. This is a Brooklyn-ified, Babel-ified tropical cocktail from their menu that's nutty, spicy, and fruity. Gin isn't often seen in tropical drinks because it can get easily lost among the strongly flavored ingredients common in the genre, but not Babel gin! It has a whole lot of personality and can stand up to all the big, bold flavors in this cocktail, including spiced rum and orgeat (an almond syrup commonly used in tropical cocktails).

Obeah is an African healing tradition from the Caribbean, and an Obeah woman is said to have been born with the special power to heal others. In a way, Marva and Myriam are modern-day Obeah women, bringing together their community in a restorative place.

Makes 1 drink

1 ounce Babel gin

1 ounce orgeat (page 217)

¾ ounce spiced rum, preferably Blackheart or Gary's Good

¾ ounce Donn's Mix (Babel Edition) (recipe follows)

½ ounce pamplemousse (grapefruit) liqueur

½ ounce fresh lemon juice

1 dehydrated orange half-moon, for garnish

Purple sweet potato powder, for garnish (available at
        specialty food stores or online)

Combine the gin, orgeat, spiced rum, Donn's Mix, pamplemousse liqueur, and lemon juice in a shaker tin filled with ice. Shake until chilled, then strain into Collins glass filled with crushed ice. Garnish with the dehydrated orange and a dusting of purple sweet potato powder and serve.

## DONN'S MIX (BABEL EDITION)
Makes 1 cup

½ cup fresh grapefruit juice

½ cup honey

½ teaspoon ground cinnamon

Pinch of sea salt

Combine all the ingredients in a nonreactive airtight container and stir until thoroughly combined. Cover and store in the refrigerator for up to 2 weeks.

BARTENDER, EDUCATOR, AND COFOUNDER OF SPEED RACK

# LYNNETTE MARRERO

f you had to name a Jackie of all trades in the spirits industry, it would be Lynnette Marrero. She's an award-winning bartender, cocktail consultant, spirits educator, and philanthropist, and she's worn many other hats along the way throughout her storied career. Lynnette was one of the first women to break into the boys' club of the cocktail scene in the early aughts, and ever since, she's been a leading voice for women's empowerment in hospitality.

Everything the native New Yorker does, she does with a side of Hollywood glam—probably because she got her start in musical theater. After graduating from Columbia University, Lynnette gave acting the ol' college try. "I refused to be the cliché waiter-actor for a long time," she says. Soon enough, though, she left the theater and started working in bars (it happens to more of us than you'd think). Lynnette got a job at the Flatiron Lounge, one of the main players in what's referred to as "the craft cocktail renaissance," a movement spanning from the early 2000s to the late 2010s that revived traditional recipes and methods in cocktailing. Opened in 2003, the bar was run by matriarch of the cocktail world, Julie Reiner, and was a training ground for folks who would become the city's best bartenders, including Lynnette. "What I loved about Flatiron is that it had an art deco vibe. I could dress up and feel like I had this role to play," she says. She quickly moved up the ranks, working side by side with Julie and other heavy-hitters in the biz.

While she had a starring role in the New York cocktail scene, Lynnette also served as a brand ambassador for Zacapa Rum. "I was intrigued by the opportunity to do this more formalized storytelling," she says. Working for Zacapa caused Lynnette to explore more bars around the city, where she met other incredible female bartenders. Soon Lynnette started organizing theme nights for female bartenders to do bar takeovers, cheekily called Broad Appeal.

Another leading lady in Lynnette's cast of all-stars was Ivy Mix, a fellow Julie Reiner protégé. She and Lynnette became friends, and in 2011, the two women founded Speed Rack, an all-female bartending competition that raises money for breast cancer research. "We wanted to test people in what they actually do, which was classic cocktails with speed, and we asked everyone we knew to be in it," she says. Speed Rack earned rave reviews from the jump, and is now an annual event that takes place all over the world. Lynnette has also added author to her long list of professional endeavors: In 2024, she and Ivy penned *A Quick Drink: The Speed Rack Guide to Winning Cocktails for Any Mood*. In addition to Speed Rack, Lynnette started her own company, called DrinksAt6, to educate the next generation of bartenders. She's also a founding board member of the Restaurant Workers' Community Foundation, and she's been the head of education for both Bar Convent Brooklyn and Tales of the Cocktail.

Lynnette may not have gone into musical theater, but she's certainly become a triple (or quadruple, or quintuple) threat. Today, a lot of people have multihyphenate career titles, but that wasn't always the case. Lynnette broke the mold of what a successful career in the spirits industry could look like, and has inspired others to do the same. "It challenged people's perceptions, but I've always carved my own path," she says.

# CLARA BOW

### Created by Lynnette Marrero

It's only natural that Lynnette would pull inspiration from the ultimate 1920s It girl for this cocktail. The Clara Bow is like a Whiskey Sour meets a Whiskey Smash, and has been featured on several of Lynnette's bar menus. It's tart and fruity, thanks to grenadine, a pomegranate syrup. Since some commercial grenadines are made from artificial ingredients, Lynnette says that "the key is to use a high-quality grenadine—or make it yourself. The real pomegranate notes are essential." Finally, the freshness of the mint plays off the honeysuckle notes in the elderflower liqueur. So take a cue from Lynnette, put on some red lipstick, and take a sip of that old Hollywood glamour.

### Makes 1 drink

1 ½ ounces bourbon, preferably Bulleit

¾ ounce fresh lemon juice

½ ounce St-Germain elderflower liqueur

½ ounce Grenadine (recipe follows)

5 or 6 mint leaves, plus 1 mint leaf for garnish

Combine the bourbon, lemon juice, St-Germain, grenadine, and mint leaves in a shaker tin filled with ice. Shake until chilled, then double strain into a coupe. Garnish with the mint leaf and serve.

# GRENADINE

### Makes about 2 ½ cups

2 cups pomegranate juice

1 cup sugar, preferably turbinado

Zests of 2 oranges

1 tablespoon pomegranate molasses

½ teaspoon rose water

In a medium saucepan, combine the pomegranate juice and sugar. Heat over medium heat, stirring, until the sugar has dissolved. Reduce the heat to low and cook for 10 minutes, until the syrup has reduced. Remove from the heat and add the orange zest, pomegranate molasses, and rose water. Let cool, then fine strain into a nonreactive airtight container and cover. Store in the refrigerator for up to 1 month.

SHANNON MUSTIPHER

Today, Shannon Mustipher is known as a rum expert, but she first fell in love with the craft of making drinks while working as a barista in college. "When I was pulling the espresso shot, I could look at the rate of flow and knew exactly what it was gonna taste like," she says. "That's when I knew I was in deep." Shannon and her friends would host elaborate dinner parties, and because of her barista skills, she played the honorable role of bartender. She delighted in the act of serving drinks and soon studied up on classic cocktails, experimenting with vermouth blends and nerding out on all things spirits.

In 2014, Shannon got an opportunity that would lead her career down an unexpected path. She was tasked with turning Gladys, a Caribbean restaurant in Crown Heights, Brooklyn, into a high-end rum bar. Oh, and she had one month to do it. At the time, Shannon had little experience with rum-based cocktails, but she was up for the challenge. "I dove in and tasted something like two hundred rums—it was nuts," she recalls. That deep dive opened Shannon's eyes to the vastness of rum in terms of styles and flavor profiles. "I was instantly fascinated, and continue to be to this day," she says.

A self-proclaimed "history

buff and total nerd," Shannon read everything she could about rum, including about the genre of tiki cocktails, a collection of mainly rum-based tropical-style drinks that originated in Southern California in the 1930s. "My goal from the start was to create a bar program that would really show the merits of the rum category, so I thought, 'Well, if I want to show people what this stuff can do, then I need to make some tiki drinks,'" she says. Gladys soon became known as one of the best rum bars in New York City and Shannon became one of the spirit industry's go-to authorities on rum, serving up delicious tropical libations with style and wit.

Shannon's award-winning book, *Tiki: Modern Tropical Cocktails*, was published in 2019, making her the first Black American bartender to author a cocktail book in over a century. (Yeah, you read that correctly.) Her cocktails are playful, theatrical, and imaginative, often introducing people to flavors and ingredients they might not have tasted before, like a style of Haitian rum called clairin, or calamansi juice, or avocado oil–washed tequila. "The key to making a truly special cocktail is to engage all the senses," Shannon writes in *Tiki*.

The list of Shannon's accomplishments is long: She founded Women Who Tiki, a pop-up celebrating talented female bartenders who sling tropical drinks; she partnered with spirit brand Myrtle Bank to make her own blend of Jamaican rum; and in 2020, she was honored with the Pioneer Award from Tales of the Cocktail. She even has her own line of glassware with Cocktail Kingdom, one of the industry's favorite barware manufacturers, featuring a skeleton sporting her signature haircut.

Shannon is deeply passionate, highly ambitious, and endlessly curious, and she does it all with a wink and a smile. "Some people find the sheer diversity of rum to be frustrating or confusing, but for me, there will always be something new or different to investigate," says Shannon. "It just means I'll never be bored."

# WISE GUY

### Created by Shannon Mustipher

This warming coffee old-fashioned is Shannon's go-to winter cocktail. "The first time I served it, I mixed up a bottle for a holiday party," Shannon says. "It has since become my bottle cocktail to give to friends and family." It's bold, aromatic, and slightly spicy, while also being smooth and sippable, thanks to the high-proof rum (or rye, if you prefer). Allspice dram marries beautifully with the cinnamon and cloves infused in the spiced coffee syrup. To round out the cocktail, Jägermeister, a German herbal liqueur, brings an earthiness that plays off the bittersweet coffee. The result is an outrageously tasty cocktail you'll want to sip on all winter long. (Also, not many people would be cheeky enough to contribute a drink called the Wise Guy to a book about women in spirits. Touché, Shannon.)

### Makes 1 drink

2 ounces aged rum or bottled-in-bond rye whiskey

½ ounce allspice dram

½ ounce Jägermeister

1 barspoon Spiced Coffee Syrup (recipe follows)

1 lemon twist

1 orange twist, for garnish

Combine the rum, allspice dram, Jägermeister, and coffee syrup in a rocks glass. Add a large ice cube and stir until chilled, about 20 seconds. Express the lemon twist over the drink, then discard. Garnish with the orange twist and serve.

# SPICED COFFEE SYRUP

### Makes about ¾ cup

3 or 4 cinnamon sticks

1 teaspoon whole cloves

1 cup plus 2 tablespoons cold-brew coffee

¾ cup sugar

In a medium saucepan, toast the cinnamon and cloves over medium heat until they begin to smoke, about 45 seconds. Add the coffee and bring to a simmer. Add the sugar and stir until it has dissolved. Reduce the heat to low and simmer for 15 minutes. Remove from the heat and let steep until the syrup is rich in flavor, about 3 hours. Strain the syrup into a nonreactive airtight container and cover. Store in the refrigerator for up to 2 weeks.

# CO-OWNERS OF NOBODY'S DARLING

**A**ngela Barnes first met Renauda Riddle in 2011, when they were both volunteering at an LGBTQ community center in Chicago. "We bonded over cocktails and golf," recalls Angela. "At some point, Renauda made the overture of, 'If I were to pursue acquiring a bar, would you be interested in doing it with me?'" Renauda and Angela took a big swing and, in the summer of 2021, they opened Nobody's Darling, a women-centered queer bar. It quickly became wildly popular and cemented itself as a mainstay in Chicago's queer community.

"Everything Angela and I do at the bar is something that we love," says Renauda. She wanted to have a classy, sexy space where she could curate the same types of events they hosted at the community center (fundraisers, casino nights, burlesque performances)

while Angela was looking for a laid-back vibe. Because of its place in the fairly residential neighborhood of Andersonville, they attract a lot of locals. "As two African American women in a majority white community, we weren't quite sure how we would be received," says Angela. "But we were just really, really welcomed. They've been so supportive."

Queer bars, especially lesbian bars, have been a dying breed in America since the 1980s, so opening one is subversive, even in 2021. The bar is named for the Alice Walker poem "Nobody's Darling," which serves as an ode to the outcasts who unapologetically set their own path. Angela and Renauda's goal was to create an intentionally inclusive space for those "outcasts." "As queer women, we haven't necessarily felt comfortable in a lot of bars, to be honest," says Angela. "It was so

RENAUDA RIDDLE & ANGELA BARNES

important for us to have a bar where people would feel recognized and very comfortable. Whether you're with your friends or you're alone, that you feel safe." The space is inviting and fun, with exposed brick and disco lights everywhere. Because of the welcoming atmosphere Renauda and Angela cultivated, Nobody's Darling has been lovingly dubbed "the Queer Cheers."

Since they first connected over cocktails, Angela and Renauda decided to try their hands at mixology. They developed the original cocktail menu for Nobody's Darling in Renauda's kitchen. Now with a skilled team behind the bar, Angela and Renauda aren't the mixologists, but they sign off on every iteration of the menu. The cocktails at Nobody's Darling are straightforward and delicious—the bar was a James Beard Award finalist for Outstanding Bar Program in 2022—and around 90 percent of the drinks on their menu feature a woman- or BIPOC-owned spirits brand. "Sometimes you have to say to yourself, 'Maybe I need to put the human before the dollar every once in a while,'" Renauda says.

The two women are opposite personalities. Renauda is a vivacious partygoer, regularly frequenting bars to taste new cocktails. ("I have a serious passion for cocktails," she says. "When I get a good cocktail, you'll see it on my face because it's like biting a juicy steak.") Angela is slightly more reserved, with a bone-dry sarcastic bend. ("Of course, let's open a bar during a pandemic, who wouldn't do that, that makes sense," she quips.) Like the ingredients in any good cocktail, they play off each other

and balance each other out.

Shortly after opening, Angela and Renauda expanded Nobody's Darling into the building next door. The new side of the space, which opened in the fall of 2023, gives off a more lounge-y, upscale, almost speakeasy-like vibe. It nearly doubled their capacity, and also functions as a private event room.

Even though the original Nobody's Darling is a clear hole in one, the duo are looking to bring a sister location to the Southside of Chicago. "Now that we have a following, we can go someplace that's more of a hidden gem," says Angela. "We can bring the party to an area where we can be a part of community economic development." Renauda and Angela have built a bar that encompasses all parts of hospitality, and want to spread their mission far and wide. "I'm hopeful that at some point, there'll be a Nobody's Darling in every community because it's needed," says Renauda. "Yes, we definitely need great cocktails, but we need the human element that Nobody's Darling has to bring people together."

# KAHLO MARGARITA

Created by Xavier Sumter, lead bartender at Nobody's Darling

This cocktail is a pillar of the Nobody's Darling cocktail menu. It's a love letter to Frida Kahlo, the Mexican painter whose colors were bold and whose sexuality was fluid. A classic margarita with a little twist, it's festive and spicy, with bright passion fruit flavor thanks to Chinola passion fruit liqueur. Reposado tequila gives subtle notes of vanilla and caramel (at Nobody's Darling, they use the Black-owned tequila brand Jon Basil), and the Tajín rim adds just a touch of spice to cut through the sweetness. All in all, it's a balanced, fruit-forward margarita that will bring your people together.

Makes 1 drink

Tajín, to rim the glass
1 lime wheel, for rimming the glass and garnish
1 ½ ounces reposado tequila, preferably Jon Basil
¾ ounce Chinola passion fruit liqueur
¾ ounce fresh lime juice
½ ounce triple sec
½ ounce agave syrup (page 216)

Spread some Tajín over a small plate. Wet the rim of a rocks glass with the lime wheel, then roll it in the Tajín to coat. Set aside (reserve the lime wheel for garnish). Combine all the ingredients except for the lime wheel in a shaker tin filled with ice. Shake until chilled, then strain into the prepared rocks glass over ice. Garnish with the lime wheel and serve.

**KELSEY RAMAGE**

**K**elsey Ramage talks serious trash. The Canadian mixologist is the founder and director of Trash Collective, an anti-waste drinks education platform that challenges the way the cocktail community thinks about sustainability. Growing up in a small town in British Columbia, she's always had an appreciation for the land. But Kelsey isn't your typical tree-hugging, crunchy-granola kind of gal—she's a chic, tatted-up badass who knows bars are all about having fun, while also being one of the industry's leading voices in sustainability.

After graduating from college, Kelsey moved to Vancouver and worked at a bistro that focused on using local produce. It was there that she sank into the world of cocktails, learning from the kitchen and chefs, incorporating culinary aspects into her drink creations. Kelsey soon decided to go all in on her new career. In 2014, she sold everything she owned and moved to London to work at award-winning (now-closed) cocktail bar Dandelyan, eventually becoming their head bartender. "We were encouraged to use what we already had in house, we were using one ingredient multiple different ways," Kelsey explains. "It changed the way I approached cocktail creation." She and fellow bartender Iain Griffiths came up with the idea for a cocktail pop-up called Trash Tiki, with the goal of making tropical cocktails less wasteful. "We wanted to show people that one of the most difficult styles of drinks can be made with a little bit more respect for the ingredients that go in there."

For the pop-ups, Kelsey and

lain sourced ingredients that were essentially waste products, like coffee grounds, lime husks, and watermelon rinds. "We would go into bars or restaurants and be like, 'What are you throwing away?'" she says. The pop-ups were incredibly successful, and their work was so well-received by the industry that they published their database of recipes online; it still serves as an important resource for bartenders around the world.

Kelsey evolved Trash Tiki into Trash Collective in 2022, allowing her to experiment with more styles of drinks and add a consulting and educational component. "The main reason was to elevate everything and make it a more all-encompassing,

sustainability platform," she says. Kelsey has designed cocktail menus and drink programs for some of the world's best bars and restaurants, and Trash Collective is now the sustainability ambassador for the large spirits company Pernod Ricard.

Bars produce massive amounts of waste every night but thankfully, there are people like Kelsey working toward reducing the industry's environmental impact, and she's inspired others to get in the sustainability game. "Now people have a greater understanding of it and are getting interested in it, and brands are backing that side of the industry as well," says Kelsey. "It's nice to feel like you're not the only one trying to push this envelope."

# BEST DAMN BELLINI
### Created by Kelsey Ramage

This cocktail was on the menu at Supernova, a bar Kelsey helped open in Toronto in 2019. It's a glimpse into how bartenders can best harness their skills by using every part of an ingredient. "We focused on seasonality and respect for ingredients at the time, and we wanted to take full advantage of peach season," Kelsey says. The miso syrup adds a mouthwatering umami note that balances out the sweetness of the peach wine. Kelsey's Bellini takes a lot of prep time, but the results are worth it—it truly is the best damn Bellini!

Makes 1 drink

1½ ounces Peach Wine (recipe follows)

½ ounce Miso Syrup (recipe follows)

¼ ounce fresh lemon juice

2 ounces Prosecco

Combine all the ingredients in a mixing glass filled with ice. Stir until chilled, then strain into a flute or small wineglass and serve.

# PEACH WINE
### Makes about 2 liters

2.2 pounds (about 6 medium) unpeeled peaches, pitted
and coarsely chopped

.66 pound (about 1 ⅓ cups) sugar

.5 gram (about ½ teaspoon) Lalvin EC-1118 yeast

Thoroughly clean all your equipment. Blend peaches in a blender, then put in your fermentation vessel, such as a wide-mouth glass jar. Dissolve the sugar in 4 cups room-temperature water, then add to the peach mixture. Activate the yeast by dissolving into 2 ounces room-temperature water and let stand for 20 minutes. Add the yeast mixture to the peach mixture and close the vessel with an airlock. Ferment for 3 to 7 days, tasting regularly. Fine strain the liquid into a nonreactive container, then strain again through a coffee filter into a nonreactive airtight container and cover. Store in the refrigerator for up to 1 month.

# MISO SYRUP
### Makes about 1 quart

⅓ cup white miso paste

1.3 pounds (about 3 cups) sugar

In a small saucepan, bring 3 cups water to a boil over medium heat. Add the miso and whisk to thoroughly dissolve it, then reduce the heat and simmer for 5 minutes. Remove from the heat and allow to cool for 10 minutes. Strain through a fine-mesh strainer, then strain again through a coffee filter into a nonreactive airtight container. Add the sugar and whisk to dissolve, then cover the container. Store in the refrigerator for up to 3 weeks.

**MISTY KALKOFEN**

**E**ducation is Misty Kalkofen's vocation. Now a veteran in the spirits industry for over twenty years, she was one of the first female mixologists to rise to prominence. Though she hung up her shakers a while back, she's dedicated to educating other hospitality professionals in so many realms: agave spirits, mental health resources, women's history in bartending. Misty is like the coolest professor you'll ever have, even if she doesn't work in academia, like she once thought she would.

Misty first got behind the bar while getting her master's degree in theology at Harvard Divinity School, when she was cocktail waitressing at a music club to make money. "One night a bartender no-called, no-showed, so they were like, 'YOU!' And they threw me behind the bar," recalls Misty. "That was it, I was hooked." After finishing her degree, she knew her true calling was a different kind of divine spirit.

Misty worked in cocktail bars all over Boston, enlightening unsuspecting patrons about the classics. "Nobody was really interested in classic cocktails at that point in time. It was 1998, you know?" She developed a well of knowledge in obscure drinks, but also had fun creatively, and soon became known for her innovative libations. "There was this great group of really smart Harvard folks who would come in every Sunday with what they called, 'the garnish challenge,'" she recalls. "They would bring in random things, like circus peanuts, and say, 'Okay, can you make me a cocktail with this as the garnish?' I would look forward to it." Misty quickly earned her reputation as one of the best bartenders in town.

In 2008, Ron Cooper, the founder of Del Maguey Single Village Mezcal, was looking for someone to help get his brand off the ground. A mutual friend told him that Misty was the one. "He rolled in with a friend one Friday night, and he goes, 'We'll take two tequila cocktails of your choice,'" says Misty. "And I was like, 'Who is this guy?' Because there wasn't an agave renaissance yet." Ron was impressed by her drinks, so he poured her some of his mezcal. "He kept talking about the rituals surrounding mezcal and how it's integrated into the cultural history of the people who make it," she says. "Considering what I'd studied, that resonated with me in a really strong way." The following year, she went to Oaxaca for the first time with Ron and sixteen other bartenders, all men. "It made such an impression on me, to meet the families in the villages and see how devoted they are to the spirit," she says. When Misty returned to Boston, she was inspired to spread the good word of mezcal. She went around the country teaching people about the spirit—a tall order in the United States in the early 2010s, where mezcal was still relatively unknown.

Edifying the masses about mezcal wasn't Misty's only endeavor in spirits education. She and her friend, Kirsten "Kitty" Amann, started the Boston chapter of LUPEC (which is *not* a religious organization, but an acronym for Ladies United for the Preservation of Endangered Cocktails). They wrote weekly pieces about women in history with corresponding classic cocktail recipes, and made several attempts to turn their column into a book deal. "We got turned down right and left. We were told it was 'too niche,'" Misty recalls. It finally happened in 2016, and within a few months, Misty and Kitty submitted the manuscript for *Drinking Like Ladies*. "Every time Kitty and I thought that we weren't going to be able to do it, we would go back and read all of the rejection letters," says Misty. "I was like, 'We're doing this, no matter what.'"

Misty pivoted to not-for-profit pedagogic work. She serves as an education consultant at Another Round Another Rally, a nonprofit that provides financial and educational resources for the hospitality industry. She has also run a women's mentorship program, led educational trips, and organized seminars about mental health for hospitality professionals.

An advocate for her own community, as well as others, Misty is still super passionate about mezcal, especially promoting female producers.

She helped organize Mujer Agave, the first mezcal festival put on by women in Oaxaca. "So many cool women were there doing seminars on methanol and fermentation and all that stuff. It was so inspiring, listening to them talk about making mezcal from the perspective of a woman, rather than all the dudes that I always hear talk about it," Misty says. "Every time I start to think, 'Oh, too niche?' Well, fuck those guys. We'll do it ourselves."

# DREAM OF THE CLOUD FOREST

### Created by Misty Kalkofen

Del Maguey develops each of their mezcals in a single village, and Santo Domingo Albarradas was the first village Misty visited on her inaugural trip to Oaxaca in 2009. "The family in Santo Domingo Albarradas is very dear to me, so I'm thrilled to be able to include their mezcal in my cocktail," she says. The production of this mezcal has always been a family affair, with both men and women participating in the process. Misty has fond memories of sitting around the palenque with the family and eating bananas from their trees, so she uses banana liqueur to evoke the semi-tropical environment. A touch of fino sherry is the bridge between the smoky mezcal and the fruity banana. "The orange twist brings out a pine note in the cocktail, a perfect nod to the mountainous pine forests you have to drive through to reach the village," she says.

### Makes 1 drink

Absinthe, to rinse the glass (see page 15)

2 ounces Del Maguey Santo Domingo Albarradas mezcal

½ ounce banana liqueur, preferably Cartron Banane

¼ ounce fino sherry

1 orange twist, for garnish

Rinse a Nick and Nora glass with the absinthe. Combine the mezcal, banana liqueur, and sherry in a mixing glass filled with ice. Stir until chilled, then strain into the prepared glass. Garnish with the orange twist and serve.

**TALIA BAIOCCHI**

I f you're wondering what you should have to drink, ask Talia Baiocchi. She's the founder and editor in chief of *Punch*, a highly esteemed digital magazine and media brand that serves as one of the spirits industry's go-to sources for recipes, news, buying guides, think pieces, and more. This would be impressive enough on its own, but *Punch* was one of the first publications dedicated to all things drinks, founded at a time when beverage writing was relegated to the back of a magazine you'd find in a grocery store checkout line. And Talia started this groundbreaking media outlet before she had even turned thirty.

Talia first fell in love with wine while working as a host at a restaurant during college. After graduating in 2006 with a journalism degree, she took a leap of faith and booked a one-way ticket to Italy to work as a harvest intern with a producer in Piedmont making Barolo. "Then I just traveled to every wine region I could until I ran out of money," she recalls. After working in fine wine sales for a few years once she moved back to New York ("I quite literally went on Craigslist and typed in 'wine'"), Talia started writing about wine for high-profile publications, and was appointed the very first wine editor for Eater New York. In 2011, *Time Out Magazine* named her one of

New York's "New Wine Prophets." She was twenty-six.

In 2012, Talia was approached by Aaron Wehner, a publisher at Ten Speed Press. "He was like, 'Hey, seems like sherry's becoming a thing and I know you're really into it. Would you want to write a book about it?'" While she was working on *Sherry*, Aaron came to her again and asked if she wanted to launch a website. It's pretty remarkable to be asked to write a book, then be asked to launch a website, let alone to actually do both at the same time. But if anyone was up to the task, it was Talia.

Teaming up with her friend, writer Leslie Pariseau, Talia started *Punch*. "It was so grassroots. We worked out of my living room for two years, just us," she says. "That early partnership and creative synergy that Leslie and I had in the beginning built the foundation of what *Punch* still is today." Talia and Leslie wanted to cover all styles of alcohol, recognizing that the audiences for beer, wine, and cocktails were beginning to converge. They also knew they wanted to provide serious journalism about beverages, rather than just recipes or fluff pieces. "We wanted to contextualize drinks and prove that they have the same cultural significance as food," she says.

*Punch* officially launched in 2013 and was an instant success. In addition to a huge database of cocktail recipes, *Punch* has published pieces about the latest drink trends, interviews with dive bar bouncers, a feature story about the history of binge-drinking, and a satirical eulogy for the tiny clothespin garnish, just to name a few. And not only was one of the most important and respected drinks media outlets founded by women—it's also run by women. The full-time staff of *Punch* is made up entirely of women and nonbinary folks, and has been for many years. Along with her job as *Punch*'s editor in chief, Talia has penned a few books, three of which have been nominated for James Beard Awards.

Saying yes and emphatically throwing herself into everything she did has led her to become one of the beverage industry's most prominent voices. May we all take some notes from Talia's confidence, assuredness, and ambition in following the things we love!

# PUNCH HOUSE SPRITZ

From *Spritz: Italy's Most Iconic Aperitivo Cocktail, with Recipes*
Created by Talia Baiocchi and Leslie Pariseau

Talia is "somebody who always orders the crushable pink drink," and that's exactly what this cocktail is. It's a delicious low-ABV Italian aperitivo that is refreshing, juicy, bitter, and bubbly—everything you want from a good summer spritz. Cocchi Americano brings the bitter note, while fresh grapefruit juice adds a nice tartness, and both play off Lambrusco's delightful ripe-berry flavor.

Makes 1 drink

2 ounces Cocchi Americano

4 ounces Lini 910 Labrusca Lambrusco Rosé

1 ounce fresh grapefruit juice

1 ounce soda water

1 grapefruit half-wheel, for garnish

Combine the Cocchi, Lambrusco, grapefruit juice, and soda water in an ice-filled rocks glass or wineglass and stir. Garnish with the grapefruit half-wheel and serve.

LP O'BRIEN

Lauren Paylor "LP" O'Brien is an award-winning Afro-Latina mixologist who looks to provide cultural experiences and build community through cocktails. As an innovative entrepreneur in the beverage space, LP's main goal has always been to create diverse and inclusive spaces that promote wellness in the industry. And that's a tricky feat in a business with so much emphasis on drinking and nightlife.

Born in the Bronx, LP moved to Washington, DC, in 2010 to attend nursing school. She became a regular at The Passenger, where she would sit at the bar and do her homework. LP admired how the bartenders interacted with their guests, "primarily because they took such great care of me." LP loved that the staff took the time to cater the experience to each person at the bar. "I always knew that I wanted to connect with people, and that seemed so much more fun than what I was doing at the time," she says.

So LP went from hospitals to hospitality. She worked in all facets of the field, and once she knew hospitality was her destiny she wanted to find her rightful place in it—one that let her shine *and* best served her well-being. "How do I take the things that I love so much about this sector and turn it into something that's sustainable for me, but also something that truly aligns with what I want to do?" In 2016, she founded LP Drinks, a beverage agency that focuses on curating experiences using cocktails as a canvas. "It's so rewarding to be in a position where I can travel and immerse myself and then bring those experiences to others."

LP's cocktail creations are about evoking emotions, and she takes all five senses into account. "It's about finding authentic ways to tie all of the elements back into the story I'm telling." She created Bodega Culture, a cocktail pop-up that has traveled around the country and celebrates New York bodegas. Not only are the drinks inspired by a bodega, but the space is fully transformed to emulate one. LP makes sure to highlight snacks from BIPOC makers, donating part of the pop-up's proceeds to an organization that focuses on prison reform.

Furthering her global reach, LP competed on season one of Netflix's *Drink Masters*. The reality show featured twelve of North America's most talented bartenders, and (spoiler alert!) LP took home the main prize.

"I wanted to go out there, be authentically myself, and hopefully inspire someone along the way," she says. One of her skills that really wowed the judges was her ability to make low- and no-alcohol cocktails that felt just as special as their alcoholic counterparts. "If you can make a drink that's delicious with no alcohol, then you can absolutely make a drink with alcohol," says LP. "It really forces you to have a very good understanding of flavor and texture."

LP prioritizes health and wellness throughout the hospitality field. For her, that means taking care of herself personally, but also looking out for the people in her orbit. She is honest, intentional, and has a unique ability to always do what's best for *her*, which in turn inspires others to do the same. "You're not going to make everyone happy," she says, "but when we stop caring so much about the noise, the work that we're able to create can become so much more impactful."

# BERRY SMASH

### Created by LP O'Brien

This cocktail has been featured on LP's Bodega Culture menu. "I wanted to challenge the statement that nonalcoholic pink drinks are too sweet and unbalanced," she says. Perfect on a hot summer's day, it's fruity and refreshing, but has so much going on. LP uses a base of Seedlip Garden 108, an herbaceous nonalcoholic spirit, and hibiscus tea, giving the cocktail a lovely verdant note. The three-berry combo makes the cocktail rich and full of fresh berry flavor, while the ginger beer adds a subtle spice. "It's a well-balanced nonalcoholic beverage that has complexity, is aesthetically pleasing, *and* is delicious," LP says.

### Makes 1 drink

1 ounce Seedlip Garden 108

1 ounce Hibiscus Tea (recipe follows)

¾ ounce fresh lemon juice

¾ ounce Berry Syrup (recipe follows)

2 ounces ginger beer

1 mint sprig, for garnish

Combine the Seedlip, tea, lemon juice, and berry syrup in a shaker tin filled with ice. Shake until chilled, then strain into an ice-filled Collins glass. Top with the ginger beer, garnish with the mint sprig, and serve.

## HIBISCUS TEA

### Makes 1 cup

2 tablespoons dried hibiscus flowers

Combine the hibiscus flowers and 1 cup hot water in a heatproof container and steep for 5 minutes. Strain into a nonreactive airtight container and let cool. Cover and store in the refrigerator for up to 1 month.

## BERRY SYRUP

### Makes 2 cups

⅔ cup raspberries

½ cup blueberries

⅔ cup strawberries, hulled and sliced

1 cup cane sugar

In a sturdy medium container, muddle the berries with the sugar and let stand for 1 hour. Transfer the mixture to a blender, add ¼ cup water, and blend until smooth. Fine strain into a nonreactive airtight container and cover. Store in the refrigerator for up to 1 week.

**CHOCKIE TOM**

**A**s a bartender and activist, Chockie Tom is a fearless champion for the Indigenous hospitality community. She is focused on dismantling colonial stereotypes around tropical cocktails and amplifying other Indigenous voices within the drinks industry. "Starting these conversations and creating these social spaces where people can be welcomed is super important because bars and taverns are the living rooms of the world."

Before starting her career in hospitality, the native Californian (whose heritage includes Indigenous Pomo and Walker River Paiute) spent some time in the tattoo industry. "I really liked how all of society went through tattoo shops,

and there was a certain amount of respect where, if you were being a terrible customer, they could tell you to fuck off, essentially," says Chockie. "I saw a similar power dynamic with bartending."

Chockie has made a name for herself in the industry, working at high-end cocktail bars in New York City, building bar programs, and participating in cocktail competitions. She first tended bar at various dives and music venues, then transitioned to creating craft cocktails. As she worked her way up, Chockie saw a lack of both Indigenous representation and acknowledgment of Indigenous contributions to the drink and food space. She wanted to use her platform to spread awareness and tell stories through her cocktails. "On a cultural level for me, oral history is very strong. If your grandmother told a story of how this food came about, why not do the same with a cocktail?" she says. Chockie is intentional with every aspect of her cocktail making, from the flavor profile to the drink name to the glassware. She aims to utilize ingredients native to the Americas, like tomatoes, chiles, corn, chocolate, even wine.

In 2019, Chockie cofounded Doommersive with fellow bartender Austin Hartman. Doommersive is a cocktail pop-up that calls attention to the problematic nature of tiki bars by challenging their established aesthetic. So instead of hula girls and totems, Chockie and Austin employ satanic and heavy metal imagery. Rather than serving cocktails in glassware shaped like tiki heads, they use demonic cat mugs, with inverted crosses painted on their foreheads and eyes bleeding black tears. "It was an Indigenous response to dealing with a lifetime of cultural appropriation," says Chockie. "Having the opportunity to do something subversive and thoughtful, but also with a lot of shock value, really appealed to me." In addition to shaking up delicious drinks, Doommersive pop-ups are what Chockie calls "fund-ragers," raising money for charities that aid the BIPOC community.

In addition to Doommersive, Chockie has written articles for various drinks publications and organized several all-Indigenous panels at Tales of the Cocktail. Educating non-Indigenous people is a crucial part of what Chockie does, but she is also just as passionate about supporting other Indigenous bartenders, encouraging them to use cocktails to tell their own stories. "I want to keep pushing these conversations until it becomes status quo," she says. "I used to do it to see if I could. Now I can just straight-up do it."

# BURNING INTO THE SEA

Created by Chockie Tom

For this recipe, Chockie took inspiration from the Penicillin, a modern classic cocktail made of Scotch, ginger, lemon, and honey. "I wanted to use medicinal ingredients from an Indigenous palate," she says. Del Maguey Chichicapa mezcal provides a base of citrus and smoke that plays off the pine liqueur. "Spruce tips and other parts of the pine tree were important parts of Indigenous diets," says Chockie. Nori nods to the use of seaweed in coastal cuisine, and Chockie combines it with pink peppercorns, which grew all over her yard when she was a kid. "Despite all the ingredients having medicinal properties, the concept of nostalgia and good feelings is the medicine I want this cocktail to represent," she says.

Chockie recommends using Super Juice (a sustainable juice alternative developed by fellow Indigenous bartender Nickle Morris) in this cocktail. It's easy to make and gives you a lot more juice than using citrus fruit alone, but regular ol' freshly squeezed lemon juice can be substituted.

Makes 1 drink

2 ounces mezcal, preferably Del Maguey Chichicapa

¾ ounce Nori-Peppercorn Honey (recipe follows)

¾ ounce Super Juice (page 218)

¼ ounce pine liqueur

1 piece of honeycomb, for garnish

Combine the mezcal, honey, Super Juice, and pine liqueur in a shaker tin filled with ice. Shake until chilled, then strain into a rocks glass over a big ice cube. Garnish with the honeycomb and serve.

## NORI-PEPPERCORN HONEY

Makes about 1 cup

½ cup clover honey

½ cup sugar

½ nori sheet, roughly broken up into small pieces

2 tablespoons whole pink peppercorns

In a small saucepan, combine ½ cup water, the honey, sugar, and nori pieces. Gently stir, then bring to a boil over medium heat. Immediately remove from the heat and add the peppercorns. Let stand for 30 minutes, then fine strain into a nonreactive airtight container and cover. Store in the refrigerator for up to 1 week.

# OWNER OF THE SPORTS BRA

**JENNY NGUYEN**

There's a bar in Portland, Oregon, where jersey-clad patrons are chowing down on burgers while watching a game, sports memorabilia lines the walls, and the soundtrack is filled with jock jams. But this isn't your typical sports bar. It's the Sports Bra, the first bar in America dedicated solely to women's sports, dreamed up by chef and lifelong sports fan, Jenny Nguyen. The Sports Bra is more than just a bar—it's a safe space for the queer community, a celebration of female athletes, a physical embodiment of the fight to close the gender pay gap in sports. And it's a slam dunk.

A first-generation Vietnamese American, Jenny was born and raised in Portland. Her first love was basketball, and she had every intention of becoming a professional baller—until she tore her ACL right before starting college. Her sense of identity was thrown into disarray, but she soon found a new passion. "I started cooking in college, out of what felt like necessity, and I realized that I really loved it," she says. She went to culinary school and worked in fine-dining restaurants, climbing the ladder from prep cook all the way up to executive chef.

Basketball remained a big part of Jenny's life, shooting hoops and

watching the WNBA with friends. The idea of the Sports Bra had been a running joke among her crew, a fantasyland where women's sports would always be on TV, since they regularly had difficulty finding a bar that would show a women's sporting event, let alone with sound. "There is a lack of representation, lack of investment, just overall inequities for women in the sports field," says Jenny. "Having a place to celebrate women's sports, a place where you can be very public about it, would be awesome."

Jenny chose to open the Sports Bra (or "The Bra," as she calls it) in Northeast Portland, about a mile and a half from her childhood home. She initially conceived of it as a bar to support women and girls in sports, but as a queer woman of color, she inherently created a place that represents her and her values. "I wanted to build a space where everybody felt welcome. Anyone could walk in here and feel like they belong," she says. The Sports Bra officially had its tip-off in April 2022 and immediately

attracted an array of people with a large contingent from the LGBTQ community. "I grossly underestimated the success of the Bra," Jenny recalls.

Because she's a chef, Jenny designed the food menu. They've got standard pub grub (some dishes have a Vietnamese twist as a nod to her heritage), and a large selection of signature cocktails. Jenny follows through on the bar's cheeky motto—"We support women"—in the food and beverage department, sourcing products from female farmers and women-owned businesses. Patrons can also add a "side of equity" to their check, a five-dollar donation to the Voice in Sport Foundation, an organization calling for equal pay in sports.

The Sports Bra is decidedly kid-friendly—not exactly the MO for most bars. But for Jenny, being welcoming to families was paramount. "What if my parents had taken me to the Sports Bra when I was a kid? How much of an impact would that have made to be in a space where

I could see women playing the sport that I love, then look around and see people watching and celebrating that?" says Jenny. "I thought, 'If I can get one kid in here that feels that way, this whole thing would be worth it.'" While it took Jenny's parents a while to come around to supporting her new venture, they are now a permanent fixture at the Bra, commonly referred to by the staff as "Mom and Dad."

When working on her initial business plan, Jenny came across a question in an application about naming her competitors. "I wrote one sentence and it said, 'The only competition is the status quo.'" And now the bar is becoming a *part* of the status quo: Jenny is franchising the Sports Bra for national expansion, thanks to an investment from Reddit cofounder Alexis Ohanian, also known as Mr. Serena Williams.

Jenny is a true badass, taking a risky jump shot that could've been an air ball. But with the Sports Bra, it's been nothin' but net.

# TITLE IX

Created by Mal Otten and Brooke McKinnon, bar lead and bartender, respectively, at Freeland Spirits (see page 74)

This cocktail from the Sports Bra menu, a collaboration with Freeland Spirits, is fruity yet still spirit-forward; a refreshing sipper to enjoy while you're cheering on your favorite team. The drink's name refers to the 1972 landmark civil rights law that gave women the right to equal opportunities in education—including athletics. It's a delightful take on a mint julep (the beloved cocktail of the Kentucky Derby) where fresh mint mingles with luscious peach liqueur, and both support the sweet and velvety bourbon.

At the Sports Bra, they use products from two Portland-based distilleries: bourbon from Freeland Spirits and Stone Barn Brandyworks's Peach Rock and Rye, a peach-flavored, whiskey-based liqueur. At 33% ABV, it's stronger than other peach liqueurs, so if you can't find it, I recommend dialing back the amount of simple syrup to your taste.

Makes 1 drink

5 mint leaves, plus 1 mint leaf for garnish

1½ ounces bourbon, preferably Freeland Spirits

¾ ounce peach liqueur, preferably Stone Barn Brandyworks Peach Rock and Rye

½ ounce simple syrup (page 218)

Gently muddle the mint leaves in the bottom of a shaker tin, then add the bourbon, peach liqueur, and simple syrup and fill with ice. Shake until chilled, then pour into a rocks glass. Garnish with the remaining mint leaf and serve.

**W**omen have always been resourceful, often because they had to be. (Necessity is the *mother* of invention, after all.) Those beer-brewing women in the Middle Ages sold their ale out of their homes, effectively starting the very first alehouses. Women were integral to smuggling booze during Prohibition—female bootleggers are believed to have sold five times more than their male counterparts. Of course, alcohol is profitable, and throughout history, men have viewed women who have their own capital as a threat. Much to men's chagrin, women across time have always discovered new ways to gain autonomy in a patriarchal society.

In the modern world, women can open bar tabs and incorporate companies. But the truth is that businesses founded solely by women receive less than 3 percent of all venture capital investments, and the numbers get even more dismal when it comes to companies owned by women of color. Capital is necessary when starting a new enterprise, and women everywhere often have to fight an uphill battle to get their companies off the ground. And even if a woman isn't starting her own business, the reality for women in the workplace can still be grim. Women are often paid less than men for doing the same work (the gender wage gap in America has barely narrowed in decades), and women are still largely underrepresented in leadership roles: As of 2023, women run 10 percent of Fortune 500 companies, meaning there are finally now more female CEOs than ones named John (literally).

Just like most other industries, the spirits industry is tough for women to break into. But fear not, because just like their predecessors, many women are finding independence, making waves, and creating space for themselves and other women in spirits. Every woman in this book is a trailblazer in some way, but the vanguard in this section have forged their own paths in the spirits industry. They are inspiring and groundbreaking, and they make us truly excited about the future of spirits.

# TRAILBLAZERS

CO-OWNER AND "CHIEF BRAND DEVELOPMENT QUEEN" OF SAINT LUNA MOONSHINE

# AUBREY SLATER

**A**ubrey Slater has lived many lives. Both a hospitality veteran and an actual veteran (she's a former Marine), she has a storied history serving up drinks. Since Aubrey's first gig tending bar in 1994, she's worked in fine-dining restaurants, cheeseburger chains, wineries, cruise ships, nightclubs, and cocktail bars. She's managed bar programs for prominent restaurateurs across the country, from Maui to San Francisco to New York. Oh, and she's also an advanced-level sommelier. As if all that weren't enough, Aubrey has made history as the first transgender woman ever to own a liquor company. She's skyrocketed her brand, Saint Luna Moonshine (and the genre of moonshine itself), into the world of premium craft liquor. "If you create your own spirit category, then you don't have to worry about telling people *how* your product is different," she says. "It just *is* different."

Aubrey carries herself with confidence and ease, but that wasn't always the case. "Being transgendered and dealing with it all my life, I'd always had this darkness," says Aubrey. "I was very self-loathing; I was very self-destructive." After struggling with homelessness and battling a drug addiction, Aubrey moved to New York City in 2012 to find a supportive community and start her transition. "I went out into the world to interview for jobs as Aubrey for the first time," she says. "When I finally got a job as my true self, it was like starting anew."

Soon Aubrey began making her mark on the New York cocktail scene. In 2019, she tended bar at three upscale, high-volume cocktail bars run by the Overthrow Hospitality group. Within a few months, she climbed the ranks to assistant general manager, then general manager and beverage director—of all three bars. Under her direction, they were all wildly successful. Aubrey truly was kicking ass and taking names.

One night, while working at one of the bars she was managing, Aubrey met David Suk, founder of a new small-batch moonshine brand called Saint Luna. They quickly became good friends, and in 2021, he invited her on a sales trip to Pittsburgh. With her charisma and industry acumen, Aubrey opened ten new accounts in two days. David immediately asked her to be his business partner, giving her a decision to make: She could go back to working for other people, or she could take control of her own destiny. "Next thing you know, I'm just bouncing around New York City trying to sell this moonshine to people," she recalls.

"Moonshine" is a catchall term for high-proof liquor that was traditionally made illegally, with its name deriving from producers distilling at night in order to avoid being discovered. Commercial moonshine (which is generally clear and unaged) can now be produced legally, but it still doesn't have the best reputation. "Most people see moonshine and think Ole Smoky in a mason jar filled with apple pie flavor," says Aubrey. But premium moonshine is not an oxymoron. "We're trying to elevate the whole spirit category and give it its rightful due—what it deserves," she says.

Saint Luna is distilled in Tennessee from 95 percent molasses and 5 percent rye. It hits a lot of categories of flavor: smokiness, spiciness, sweetness. The sugarcane base lends itself to tropical and fruit-forward flavors, but the sharpness of the rye means it's great for more spirit-forward cocktails. At 50% ABV, Saint Luna Moonshine is no joke, but it's still insanely drinkable. "Pretty little poison, that's what I like to call it," says Aubrey. "Because once you put it in a cocktail, that bite goes away." Both Aubrey and Saint Luna have garnered well-deserved attention: In 2022, for example, Aubrey was chosen for *Wine Enthusiast*'s Future 40 list.

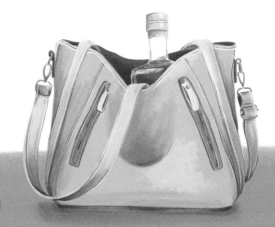

As the company's "Chief Brand Development Queen" (yes, that's her official title), Aubrey travels around the United States promoting Saint Luna. Bartenders aren't always psyched to see a liquor rep pull up a stool to peddle their wares in the middle of a shift, but that's not the case with Aubrey. She's beloved in the industry, and because she spent most of her career as a cocktail creator, her opinion about spirits is highly valued. "I look at moonshine as jazz," she says. "It's a free-form art that is at the whim of the artist."

Aubrey always carries a bottle of Saint Luna in her purse, and whenever she visits accounts or a new bar, she chats up the guests next to her, offering them a taste. (Even though Saint Luna is a legitimate company, giving people sips from a bottle that you pull out of your bag has a very old-school, illicit vibe to it.) And if there's anyone who can convince an entire country to love a misunderstood spirit just by pouring a drink, it's Aubrey.

# PRETTY LITTLE POISON

An homage to Aubrey's nickname for Saint Luna, this cocktail personifies its title: a dangerous potion in a dainty package. It's nearly all booze but doesn't look (or taste) like it. For this drink, I tapped into Saint Luna's softer, floral qualities, which play beautifully with the tropical coconut liqueur (a nod to Aubrey's brief stint in Maui). Just a touch of lemon juice adds a tart pop, and a few dashes of Peychaud's bitters give the cocktail some fruity aromatics. Finally, it's topped off with Champagne. Yes, the real stuff—it's perfectly dry, with gentle bubbles, so it doesn't drown out the flavors of the other ingredients. Plus, the Queen deserves the royal treatment, don't you think?

Makes 1 drink

1½ ounces Saint Luna Moonshine

¾ ounce coconut liqueur, preferably Kalani

¼ ounce fresh lemon juice

4 dashes Peychaud's bitters

Champagne, to top

1 grapefruit twist, for garnish

Combine the moonshine, coconut liqueur, lemon juice, and bitters in a flute. Top with Champagne and stir gently. Garnish with the grapefruit twist and serve.

# FOUNDER AND MASTER BONDER OF J.J. CORRY IRISH WHISKEY

## LOUISE McGUANE

Imagine being responsible for reviving a piece of your country's heritage. Louise McGuane can, because that's exactly what she did. With her company, J.J. Corry, Louise single-handedly recovered the extinct practice of Irish whiskey bonding. As Ireland's first modern whiskey bonder and the first female founder in the present-day Irish whiskey industry, she is innovative, passionate, and a true leader. "I have the opportunity to be a part of an ancient industry that's reinventing itself, and I'm able to pave my own way," she says.

Growing up on a farm in County Clare on the west coast of Ireland, Louise always had a passion for the drinks industry. She pursued a career in the corporate beverage world and worked for large companies like Moët Hennessy and Diageo. Even though her job took her all over the globe, she always kept an eye on the spirits industry in her home country, as well as the booming craft distillation movement in America. "I was like, that is going to happen in Ireland," says Louise. "The whole category of Irish whiskey is about to be reborn, and I want to be a part of that."

In 2012, Louise left the corporate sphere and moved back to Ireland to spend some time on her family's farm. Knowing that she would eventually inherit it ("because the Irish are very weird about land due to our history"), Louise decided she would start her own whiskey company in County Clare. As she was researching the Irish whiskey business, she came across many bottles with labels stating "J.J. Corry Whiskey Bonder." Not knowing what "whiskey bonder" meant, and not getting answers from anyone in the industry, Louise became a researcher, combing through any and all resources she could get her hands on, including the British and Irish Parliamentary Archives. Eventually, she discovered that the act of whiskey bonding was once an integral part of the Irish whiskey industry.

Whiskey bonding (not to be mistaken with American bottled-in-bond whiskey) is sourcing, maturing, and blending whiskeys from different distilleries to create new blends. During the nineteenth and twentieth centuries (considered the golden age of Irish whiskey), hundreds of distilleries were operating in Ireland. Most didn't have their own brands, so they sold their new-make whiskey wholesale to bonders, who would travel to distilleries, fill up their barrels, then take them home to age, blend, and bottle. The entire whiskey industry in Ireland collapsed in the 1930s and the few remaining distilleries cut off the bonders' supply, so the practice of whiskey bonding died.

That is, until Louise came along nearly a hundred years later, when the Irish whiskey industry was being rebuilt. (Louise's instinct about her hometown spirit was correct: In 2012, there were only three distilleries in Ireland, but as of 2023, the island is home to over forty distilleries.) Once she learned about whiskey bonding, she knew that was the direction to take. "If I'm going to contribute to the rebirth of Irish whiskey in a meaningful way, I'm going to do that because it's bringing back the heritage," says Louise. In 2015, Louise built a rackhouse and blending room on the McGuane family farm and founded J.J. Corry Irish Whiskey.

Louise's job is basically putting together a giant creative puzzle with lots of moving parts. First, she builds relationships with various distilleries around Ireland to source the liquid. She then works with coopers, wineries, and distilleries around the world and buys their casks. Her first main partnership was with several sherry bodegas in Jerez, Spain, but she also sources bourbon casks from Kentucky, rum casks from the Caribbean, and tequila casks from Jalisco. The casks are then categorized into "flavor blocks." It's like the Dewey decimal system of casks: They could be grassy, citrusy, floral, fruity, nutty. "You taste the cask and then it tells you what it is, basically," she says. By now, Louise can identify which flavor block a cask belongs to just by its smell. "I know straight away, I just go, sniff sniff. 'Right, got it, okay, you're over there.'"

The next step is to match the style of the sourced liquid to the cask. "You have to figure out, 'Okay, distillery X will go well in winery Y casks, so we'll put those together,'" Louise says. From there, the liquid is aged in the J.J. Corry rackhouse, and when the whiskey is ready, Louise begins the blending process. "I might be blending from eight different distilleries, you

know, little bits and pieces in there," she explains. "The more diverse library of flavors that you have, the more interesting the whiskey is at the end." Louise is always experimenting, as is the nature of whiskey bonding, but there are a few core products in the J.J. Corry portfolio: the Gael, the Hanson, and the Flintlock. They're all distinct but share the same house style of being "big and juicy fruit bombs."

As the only female founder of an Irish whiskey company, Louise purposely hired a majority-female team to get more women involved in the industry. "I was very intentional about creating some kind of a pipeline. The way that the industry has evolved is that there is a collegiate atmosphere, but I deal with men exclusively, pretty much," says Louise. "Somebody has to be at the other end of the spectrum, and right now, that's me. We have to create that space for women in the industry as a whole."

Bringing back an entire practice of making whiskey isn't exactly small potatoes, and Louise received pushback when J.J. Corry first launched. "I think in the beginning, people just weren't buying the concept of it," she says. "A lot of people thought it was garbage and just a marketing story." But Louise wasn't going to give up. "I've worked extremely hard to put on a pedestal what modern whiskey bonding means and should mean in

the context of the industry." She's certainly succeeded: J.J. Corry has won numerous awards and has earned its place on the shelf in the canon of great Irish whiskeys. "Now people believe, you know?"

# COUNTY CLARE SOUR

Louise describes her favorite cocktail, a classic New York Sour, as "a big guilty pleasure," but I say there's nothing to feel guilty about! A New York Sour is an egg white whiskey sour with a red wine float, so I took that formula to Ireland and made the County Clare Sour. It's the same basic structure, but uses blood orange for additional juiciness and to play off the fruity quality of J.J. Corry. The Hansen has a lot of the same characteristics as a good bourbon, since it's aged in ex-bourbon casks, so it's great in cocktails where bourbon would normally be used. Finally, the float on top is a mix of red wine and amontillado sherry, as a nod to Louise's partnership with the bodegas in Jerez. The result is a delicious cocktail that honors tradition while embracing modernity, just like Louise.

Makes 1 drink

2 ounces J.J. Corry The Hansen Irish whiskey

1 ounce fresh blood orange juice

¾ ounce fresh lemon juice

¾ ounce simple syrup (page 218)

1 large egg white

¼ ounce amontillado sherry, to float

¼ ounce red wine, to float

Combine the whiskey, blood orange juice, lemon juice, simple syrup, and egg white in a shaker tin. Dry shake (see page 15), then add ice and shake again until chilled. Double strain into a rocks glass over a big ice cube. Combine the sherry and red wine in a separate vessel, then float them over the top of the cocktail and serve.

CAROLYN KIM

awyer Carolyn Kim was looking for an easy, low-proof drink to have after work, before starting her nighttime routine with her young kids. She wanted a spirit that wouldn't knock her out, something fairly light that she could drink regularly. As a Korean American, Carolyn thought of soju, a Korean distilled spirit that tends to be lower in alcohol. "I feel like it's part of my identity, because I grew up drinking soju and had this affinity for it," says Carolyn. "But I was like, this is not good stuff. It's cheap and gets you drunk." Inspired by the booming Korean culinary scene in New York, Carolyn wanted to bring an elevated and sophisticated soju to the table, something that didn't really exist in the United States at the time. So in 2015, she and her husband, James, started their own spirits brand: Yobo, America's first craft soju. "Being a new mom, I wanted to tap into a different side of my identity," she says. "I wanted to create something, make something my own, something to add to the conversation as a Korean American."

Traditionally, soju is a spirit made in Korea, often distilled from rice or other grains. It tends to be smooth and mild, with an ABV around 30%, and it's usually consumed neat or over ice. With

Yobo, Carolyn wanted to pay respect to tradition, but put her own spin on it. Instead of rice, Yobo is made from grapes, an unusual choice for soju. But the grapes impart a flavor that isn't inherent in grains. "With grapes, you get something that's very natural, and there's that subtle, pretty fragrance to it," Carolyn says. Yobo is delicate and floral; complex yet clean. The word yobo means "honey" or "darling" in Korean and symbolizes bringing people together. It hearkens back to the way Carolyn would drink soju with friends in college, but Yobo is a high-quality, aromatic, and nuanced spirit, not a sugar bomb designed to get you intoxicated. "You can enjoy it in social gatherings with friends, or just a quiet evening by yourself," she says. "We're creating these dimensions to it, both in terms of flavor and how it's consumed."

That's not to say that Carolyn didn't have her fair share of critics. "There was some skepticism about the idea of Korean American soju. There was some resistance to doing something different," explains Carolyn. "But I never set out to do something super traditional." Well, haters be damned, because since their launch, Yobo now has multiple products. They have their flagship spirit, Yobo Soju Luxe; KTown, a line of flavored soju; Hunni, a line of canned sparkling soju; and they've collaborated with Korean American chef and *Top Chef* winner-turned-host Kristen Kish to create a line of soju apéritifs.

Yobo Soju is just as sophisticated and hardworking as Carolyn is herself. She manages to remain graceful and poised, all while juggling her company, her twin boys, and her day job—Carolyn is still a full-time lawyer working in the nonprofit sector. It has always been part of Yobo's mission to give back, donating to Asian American organizations to spread awareness about anti-Asian violence and provide aid to the AAPI community. "Alcohol's not going to save the world, but we do what we can to contribute," she says.

# GREEN LIGHT

With Carolyn's cocktail, I wanted to play off the soft, botanic elements in Yobo while keeping it low ABV. Muddling fresh, green grapes really brings out the grape notes in the spirit. Salers is a French apéritif that's earthy and vegetal but is light enough to not overpower the soju. And since elderflower is one of Carolyn's favorite ingredients, St-Germain fits right in. This is a flavorful cocktail that won't knock you out or hold you back.

Makes 1 drink

3 or 4 green grapes, plus 1 grape skewered on a cocktail
   pick, for garnish
1½ ounces Yobo Soju
½ ounce fresh lemon juice
½ ounce Salers apéritif
½ ounce St-Germain elderflower liqueur

Gently muddle the grapes in the bottom of a shaker tin. Add the soju, lemon juice, and Salers and fill with ice. Shake until chilled, then double strain into a rocks glass over ice. Garnish with the skewered grape and serve.

COCKTAIL
HISTORIAN AND
AUTHOR OF
*GIRLY DRINKS*

MALLORY O'MEARA

"If you want to know how society treats its women, all you have to do is look into the bottom of a glass," writes Mallory O'Meara in her seminal, award-winning book, *Girly Drinks: A World History of Women and Alcohol*. Published in October 2021, *Girly Drinks* is the first of its kind: an opus about the untold history of female distillers, brewers, and drinkers through the ages. There are plenty of books about cocktail history (almost all written by men), many by esteemed cocktail historians (who are almost all dudes). But it took Mallory, an outsider in the industry, to bust the category wide open and shine a light on the women who shaped how and what we drink today.

Mallory's background is in film, and she fell into being a historical writer with her debut book, *The Lady From the Black Lagoon: Hollywood Monsters and the Lost Legacy of Milicent Patrick*, about the woman who designed the infamous sea monster, and it was a friend who first turned Mallory on to the glory of cocktails. Being a naturally curious person and a self-proclaimed "huge history nerd," Mallory took a deep dive into the world of cocktails, both how to make them and the stories behind them. But the more she read, the more disappointed she got. Not only were the books written mainly by men—there was barely any mention of women. "Alcohol is the nexus of so many things in our society. I refused to believe that there weren't women involved," she says. So Mallory decided she would write the book that she wanted to read.

In the two years it took for her to research and write *Girly Drinks*, Mallory read over five hundred books. Mainly because there was so little written about women and booze, she had to find bits and pieces in a wide variety of sources: women's history books, recipe books, books on partying and feasting, articles, master's theses and PhD dissertations, academic journals, encyclopedias, even the occasional historical TV series. She was amazed by what she found, like how the first depiction of a person drinking is a woman, or how the very first brewers were women. "Some of the things that women contributed to the world, the culture and the industry of creating alcohol is essential stuff," explains Mallory. "Like, how could you leave that out!?"

One of Mallory's core discoveries was that the idea of what constitutes a "girly drink" started way earlier than the invention of the Appletini. "We take it for granted that something sweeter is more girly, and a drink that's more austere is male," Mallory says. "I was really shocked to find out that it's been going on for literally thousands of years. It's so tied to social power and patriarchy." Mallory came to the consensus that "all drinks are girly drinks" because of how important women were, and still are, in the world of alcohol.

Mallory's writing style is amiable and casual—it feels much more like talking with a friend than reading a history book. "The whole point is to bring as many eyes as I can to these women who have done amazing things, and I personally feel like you can't do that if you're writing in a very academic, dense way," she says. "Also, I like swearing a lot."

Turns out, a book like *Girly Drinks* didn't exist because Mallory needed to be the one to write it. She is a hilarious and inquisitive historian who studies the past while keeping an eye on the future. "The power of history to make you reassess the present is really important," says Mallory. "I think a lot of women have the experience of going into a bar and not feeling welcome. But now having written this book, I know that we've always belonged there. Having that history and knowing that you have a legacy is very powerful."

# FEMME FATALE

For Mallory's cocktail, it was only fitting to turn to history and riff on a cocktail that was created by a woman. Ada Coleman is considered to be the world's first female celebrity bartender. While running the American Bar at the Savoy Hotel in the early twentieth century, she invented a drink called the Hanky Panky. It's traditionally made of gin, sweet vermouth, and Fernet-Branca, an Italian amaro with a strong menthol quality. Here I swap in whiskey for the gin, because Mallory is a bourbon girl (she even jokes that bourbon, specifically Buffalo Trace, is her "platonic life partner"). Bitter Punt e Mes is the vermouth of choice, while amontillado sherry helps to balance out the forceful fernet. Finally, a few dashes of mole bitters bring a hint of spice. This drink is boozy, bitter, and complex, perfect for any woman who wants to tap into her power.

Makes 1 drink

1½ ounces bourbon, preferably Buffalo Trace

¾ ounce Punt e Mes

¼ ounce Fernet-Branca

¼ ounce amontillado sherry

3 dashes mole bitters

1 orange twist, for garnish

Combine the bourbon, Punt e Mes, fernet, sherry, and bitters in a mixing glass filled with ice. Stir until chilled, then strain into a rocks glass over a big ice cube. Garnish with the orange twist and serve.

# JACINE RUTASIKWA

**W**hen you think of a spirit made in Scotland, you probably think of Scotch whisky. Well, Jacine Rutasikwa and her husband, Paul, are trying to change that with Matugga Rum. Jacine and Paul make Jamaican-style rum with an East African influence using Scottish distilling methods. Matugga is one of the leaders of the growing Scottish rum industry, and Jacine is believed to be the United Kingdom's first Black female distillery owner. Talk about groundbreaking!

Jacine was born and raised in London with Jamaican roots, and there was always rum around the house when she was growing up.

"It was only ever Jamaican rum. It was just part of the family socializing," she says. When she met her Ugandan-born husband, Paul, his preferred tipple at the time was whisky. Soon, he fell in love with Jacine's favorite spirit (and her, of course). But when they visited Paul's family in East Africa, they had a hard time finding locally made rum. "It got us thinking, 'Where are the African spirits on the world stage?'" she recalls. The couple decided to launch their own rum brand inspired by their African heritage, designed for a whisky palate. They named it after the town in Uganda where Paul's late mother owned land. "Calling it

Matugga would keep us really rooted to the origin of our ideas, keep us rooted to home," says Jacine.

Because neither Paul nor Jacine knew anything about making spirits (he was a civil engineer; her background is in marketing and television), they moved to Scotland so Paul could study distilling at Heriot-Watt University in Edinburgh. "There weren't any other Black spirits founders that we could see in the UK at the time, and no scene around craft rum," Jacine recalls. They forged ahead anyway, building their own rum distillery in an empty industrial unit from the ground up. The husband-and-wife team are responsible for every aspect of the rum-making process, from fermentation, distillation, and maturation through to bottling and labeling. The couple sold their first batch of Matugga rum in 2018.

Matugga takes inspiration from Scotland's deep distilling heritage, while a lot of their production cues come from Jamaica. To complete what they call the "rum triad," they get all their sugarcane from Africa, with the goal of eventually developing a sugarcane plantation in Uganda to support local agricultural workers.

Jacine is proud of the progress she and Paul have made with Matugga, especially since securing initial funding wasn't easy. "It's very difficult for women to raise the investment that they need to move their business to the next level, and founders of color face a lot of challenges in accessing finance," she explains. "But we're very determined people." In addition to receiving a bank loan, Jacine and Paul raised a six-figure sum via a crowdfunding campaign, which allowed them to expand their production and distribution. That's when Jacine knew they had a community who truly believed in them and what they're all about. "We don't hide, we are never diluting ourselves. We're coming up with our London swagger and our African and Caribbean culture. You're gonna get it all in its pure, pure, pure essence," she says. "It's nice to be able to be ourselves, make the spirits that we want, be proud of our culture, and create these beautiful ways to fuse people and communities."

# GLOBETROTTER

For this cocktail, I wanted to use Matugga's spiced rum, because it's unlike any other spiced rum on the market. It has a masala chai profile, enriched with black tea, ginger, and honey. "We wanted to have a link to East Africa, and in Uganda and across the region, there's a big Indian population," says Jacine. This is a fun, tropical-style drink that leans into Jacine's sweet tooth. Passion fruit is one of the signature fruits in Uganda, and Chinola liqueur has a pure passion fruit flavor. Velvet falernum is a spiced almond liqueur from the Caribbean that goes well with the other spice notes in the cocktail, like cinnamon, allspice, and chai. The gentle smoke in the rum cuts through the sweetness, creating a refreshing, balanced cocktail that has Afro-Caribbean roots and a whole lot of swagger. So, in that vein, please serve this cocktail in your most fabulous glass and garnish elaborately!

Makes 1 drink

1½ ounces Matugga spiced rum

¾ ounce Chinola passion fruit liqueur

½ ounce fresh lime juice

½ ounce velvet falernum

¼ ounce cinnamon syrup (page 216)

¼ ounce allspice dram

1 mint crown, for garnish

1 orchid flower, for garnish

Freshly grated nutmeg, for garnish

Combine the rum, passion fruit liqueur, lime juice, velvet falernum, cinnamon syrup, and allspice dram in a shaker tin filled with ice. Shake until chilled, then strain into a ceramic mug or Collins glass filled with crushed ice. Garnish with the mint crown, orchid, and grated nutmeg and serve.

FOUNDER
OF YOLA
MEZCAL

**YOLA JIMENEZ**

orn in Oaxaca and raised in Mexico City, Yola Jimenez first got her passion for mezcal from her grandfather Luis. Luis was an avid mezcal lover, and later in his life, he started making mezcal on his farm in San Juan del Río, Oaxaca. Some of Yola's fondest childhood memories are of her grandfather drinking his mezcal with his friends, and soon she fell head over heels for the spirit herself. "I really love that first sip of mezcal," she says. "You can taste the soil in such a special way."

It was difficult to find good traditional mezcal in Mexico City in the early aughts. At that time, mezcal was only readily available in its birthplace, Oaxaca. Yola wanted to bring mezcal to Mexico City and have a similar experience with her friends as her grandfather had had with his. When she inherited her grandfather's farm in 2007, she brought back small batches of mezcal to share with her community, and eventually she started selling it to local restaurants and opened one of Mexico City's first mezcalerías.

In 2015, Yola and her business partners, Gina Correll Aglietti and Lykke Li, decided to start their own mezcal brand. "Mezcal has such a deep-rooted tradition within families. It's something that indigenous people of Oaxaca are really

proud of, and what they're doing is incredible," says Yola. "I wanted to create a system where we can keep the tradition of mezcal, have a brand, be able to export it, and provide constant, good employment. My goal has always been to try to make a difference in Oaxaca somehow."

Yola knew early on that she wanted her mezcal brand to focus on the women in Oaxaca who were actually doing the work, but who weren't getting any recognition. She wanted to address the industry's gender inequality and change the narrative that mezcal has been historically male-dominated. Not only is her company female-owned, but it's entirely female-operated. Guadalupe Bautista is their maestra mezcalera, or master distiller—a position traditionally held by a man. Yola Mezcal is distilled and bottled in their palenque, or distillery, by an all-female team who receive direct pay, fair wages, and childcare. "Half of the population in ninety percent of places in the world still live under very different circumstances than men," she explains. "For me, this seems to evidently be the

most important problem that everyone should be out in the streets talking about."

Luis passed down the mezcal recipe that Yola uses for her flagship spirit. It's made from two types of agave plants: espadín and madrecuixe. Espadín is the most common agave varietal used in mezcal production because it can be farmed and takes a relatively short time to mature (about six to eight years). Madrecuixe, on the other hand, is a wild varietal and takes between twelve and eighteen years to reach full maturity. Mezcal's increased international popularity has put extreme stress on Mexico's ecosystem. "We don't use a lot of madrecuixe because the way that wild agaves are being used is incredibly problematic, and I don't want to be part of that system," Yola says. Instead, she gets all her agave plants from one family, and is conscious of how much they're harvesting, always planting back the same amount of agave as they collect. Yola Mezcal isn't super smoky; instead, it tastes complex and soft, grassy and floral, a spirit for both mezcal novices and connoisseurs.

Yola is redefining and reclaiming space for women in mezcal. She's drawing a new road map for how to honor the traditions of a spirit while also addressing its pitfalls. "You can see the difference that has happened in a generation of young women having employment, having direct pay, knowing that they can be mezcaleras," she says. "Hopefully we can start working with all these younger mezcaleras, start promoting their work, and do special editions in the palenque. That's my dream."

# CHINGONA

*Chingona* is a Spanish slang term that means "badass woman," and that certainly describes Yola. She is extremely proud of her Oaxacan heritage, and I wanted to pay homage to that by creating a cocktail inspired by tejate, an indigenous Oaxacan street drink. Tejate is typically made with toasted corn, the pulpy pit of a sweet fruit called mamey, and rosita de cacao blossoms. (It's also traditionally made by women.) For this version, I use Nixta, a Mexican elote liqueur, as the corn element and crème de cacao for the chocolate notes—both highlight the earthiness in Yola Mezcal, which has just a gentle smokiness. Ancho Reyes is a Mexican chile liqueur that provides a touch of spice, and a whole egg is added to mimic the creaminess of the mamey pits, bringing a rich texture to the drink. Yola wanted her mezcal to work for both newbies and experts of the spirit, and this cocktail does that as well—it's accessible, delicious, and downright badass.

Makes 1 drink

1½ ounces Yola Mezcal
½ ounce Nixta Licor de Elote liqueur
⅓ ounce crème de cacao, preferably Tempus Fugit
⅓ ounce Ancho Reyes chile liqueur
1 large egg
Freshly grated nutmeg, for garnish

Combine the mezcal, elote liqueur, crème de cacao, chile liqueur, and egg in a shaker tin. Dry shake (see page 15), then add ice and shake again until chilled. Double strain into a coupe, garnish with nutmeg, and serve.

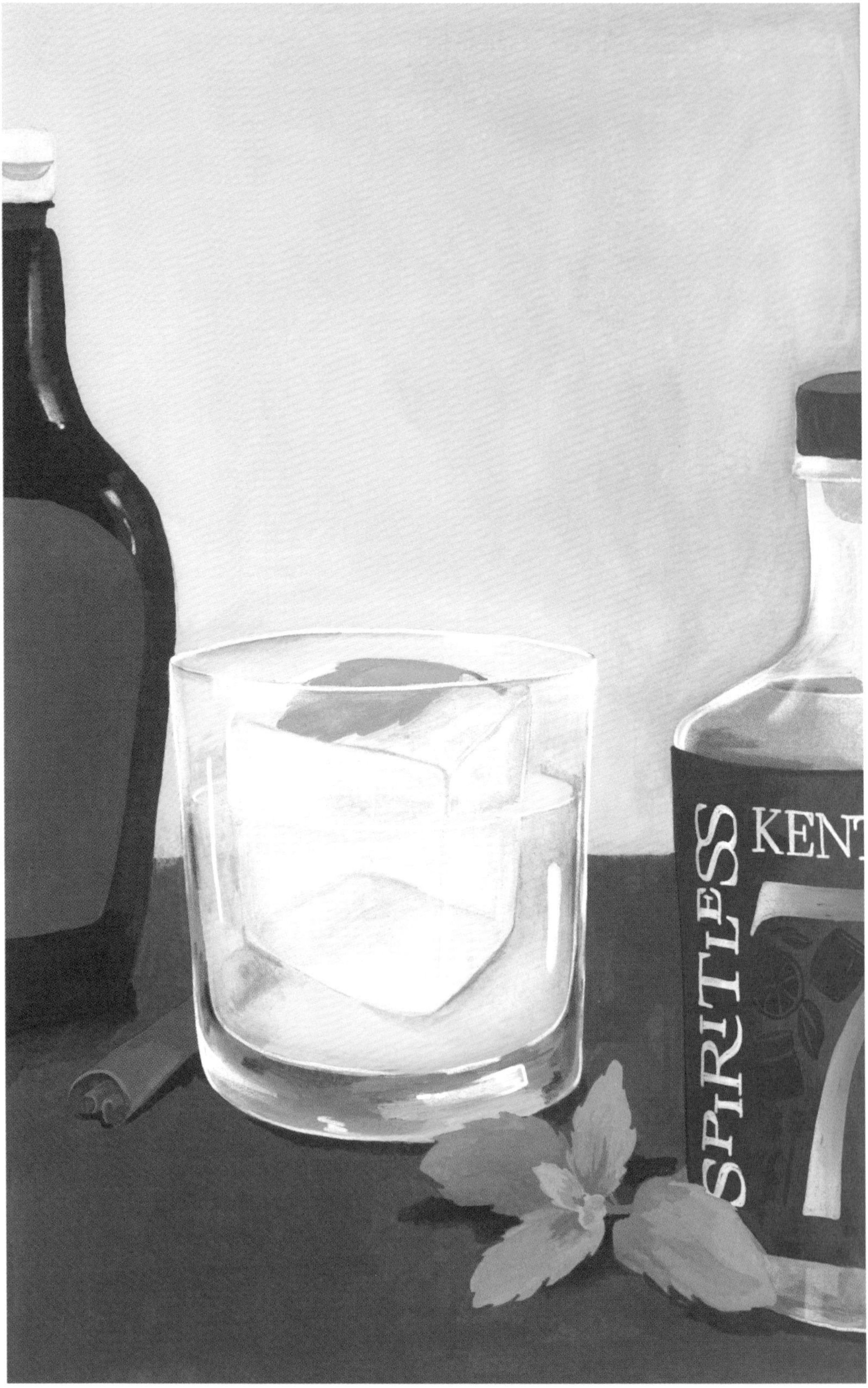
SPIRITLESS

# FOUNDERS OF SPIRITLESS

Sometimes inspiration comes when you're least expecting it. Lauren Chitwood, Abbey Ferguson, and Lexie Larsen were running a corporate event planning business in Louisville, Kentucky, and they often received last-minute requests for interesting nonalcoholic options. "I'll never forget, we were sitting in our conference room, and I was like, 'Why don't we go solve this problem?'" recalls Lauren. But they didn't just invent a new mixer or flavored seltzer. In 2019, Lauren, Abbey, and Lexie founded Spiritless, a drinks company that makes nonalcoholic spirits using a unique reverse distillation method.

Knowing that they wanted to create products that emulated premium spirits, the three women started with bourbon, an obvious choice for the Kentuckians. They began tinkering in Lauren's basement, playing around with distillation to invent something that felt and tasted like liquor, just without the alcohol. "It was probably a little dangerous, but we lived to tell the tale," says Lauren. What started as a rudimentary setup (a popcorn tin hooked up to a sump pump in a basement) ultimately resulted in their proprietary reverse distillation process and core product called Kentucky 74, one of the very first nonalcoholic bourbon alternatives on the market.

A distilled nonalcoholic spirit at first probably sounds like a contradiction, but that's exactly what Kentucky 74 is. It starts as a high-proof neutral-grain spirit combined with a blend of American oak in a range of char levels. By modulating the heat and pressure of the still, they imitate the barrel-aging process and essentially oak-infuse the distillate, resulting in an extremely strong and intensely flavored spirit. From there, the

# TRIPLE CROWN

This drink—which is like a mint julep meeting a peppermint patty—proves you really can make an elaborate cocktail without alcohol. One of the main challenges of non-alcoholic cocktails can be texture—replicating the mouthfeel of alcohol is hard!—so here's the secret: It's a clarified milk punch. Clarifying cocktails with milk removes color and tannins, leading to a drink that's beautifully clear, silky smooth, and sinfully rich without the heaviness of dairy, a great way to give a zero-proof drink that much needed body. It requires time and patience, but I promise the payoff is worth it.

The bourbon-based mint julep is the signature cocktail of the Kentucky Derby, and here, Spiritless Kentucky 74 Spiced is the prize pony. Paired with chocolate and fresh mint, it makes this luscious nonalcoholic cocktail feel like a decadent dessert without weighing you down. And since it's made as a big batch, it's perfect for a party, or to have a ready-to-pour cocktail that you can share with your friends-turned-business-partners after a long day's work.

Makes 64 ounces (about 16 cocktails)

4 cups Peppermint Tea (recipe follows)

3 cups Mint Syrup (recipe follows)

½ cup chocolate syrup, preferably Fox's U-Bet

1½ cups Spiritless Kentucky 74 Spiced

¾ cup fresh lemon juice

2 cups whole milk

Mint leaves, for garnish

Combine the tea, mint syrup, chocolate syrup, and Spiritless in a large nonreactive container. Whisk well, then cover and refrigerate overnight, or for up to 12 hours.

The next day, add the lemon juice and milk to the mixture—it will immediately begin to curdle. Give it a quick stir, then cover and let stand at room temperature for 45 minutes. Strain through a fine-mesh sieve lined with a coffee filter or cheese-cloth into a nonreactive airtight container (this will take time, so be patient!). If not serving immediately, cover and store in the refrigerator for up to 3 months.

For each serving, pour 4 ounces of the punch into a rocks glass over a big ice cube and garnish with a mint leaf.

spirit is then reverse distilled, which removes the ethanol and evaporates 95.5 percent of the alcohol. What remains is a liquid with the same vanilla and caramel notes as its boozy counterpart.

Spiritless has been a leader in the zero-proof category since it launched, all thanks to the ingenuity of these three passionate women. And Lauren, Abbey, and Lexie are making sure to pay their success forward. They started 2% for the Girls, an initiative where they donate 2 percent of sales to organizations that support young female entrepreneurs. "It just felt like, gosh, if we could have the good fortune of being able to share a little bit of this, to be able to support women's mentorship, entrepreneurship, and education, it would light us up," says Lauren.

Besides being great business partners, Lauren, Abbey, and Lexie understand each other on a personal level, as they're all working moms. (Between the three of them, they have twelve children of varying ages, so they've got their hands extremely full.) "There's a wonderful kind of empowerment in being able to work with women who are in a similar stage of life," says Lauren. "I can't imagine doing it with anybody else."

## PEPPERMINT TEA
### Makes 4 cups

6 peppermint tea bags

Place the tea bags in 4 cups hot water and steep for 10 minutes. Discard the tea bags and let the tea cool completely. Store in an airtight container in the refrigerator for up to 1 month.

## MINT SYRUP
### Makes 3 cups

10 to 12 mint sprigs
2 cups simple syrup (page 218)

Bring a small saucepan of water to a boil over medium-high heat. Fill a medium bowl with ice and water. Drop the mint sprigs into the boiling water and blanch for 15 seconds, then remove the mint and immediately plunge it into the ice water. Let cool for 1 minute, then drain the mint and pat dry with a kitchen towel. Pick the leaves and place them in a blender. Add the simple syrup and blend on high speed until fully incorporated, about 1 minute. Strain the syrup through a fine-mesh strainer into a nonreactive airtight container and cover. Store in the refrigerator for up to 2 weeks.

CEO AND HEAD DISTILLER OF CAPURRO PISCO, AND FOUNDER OF THE CRAFT SPIRITS COOPERATIVE

ROMINA SCHEUFELE

**R**omina Scheufele always had an entrepreneurial spirit. As a child in Ica, Peru, she would run around her family's farm where they raised chickens, farmed vegetables, and distilled pisco. Romina, her parents, and her siblings moved to San Francisco when she was in elementary school, and when her grandparents came to visit every summer, they brought bottles of their pisco. "I would ask my grandpa, 'Why are you bringing these bottles of alcohol?' And he would say, 'Well, this is the stuff that we make. Our family makes it this very specific way, and you can't get it here,'" explains Romina. "So as a little girl, I would say to him, 'I'm going to help you bring it to the States one day and then you won't have to bring it in your suitcase.'" And that's exactly what Romina grew up to do.

When she was in business school in 2008, Romina entered Capurro Pisco, her family's spirit, into the San Francisco World Spirits Competition without telling anyone. It won a Double Gold medal, the competition's highest honor. That was all the proof she needed to know Capurro would be successful in America. Her grandfather, Eduardo Castro Capurro, was thrilled about this new prospect but ready to retire, so he put Romina in charge. She put her business degree (and her hands) to work. "I went to Peru and just rolled up my sleeves, got my hands dirty, did the harvest, did every single part of it," Romina says. "I came back and I was like, 'Oh my gosh, I love it. I want to do this.'"

Pisco is an unaged grape brandy made in Peru and Chile. It's floral and delicate, made from several grape varieties. At Capurro, the grapes are hand-harvested only once per year, then naturally fermented into wine. From there, the pisco is distilled in a copper pot still, then rested for at least a year in stainless steel. This resting time is crucial to the quality of the spirit. "It makes the product more unctuous, it has more texture, it makes the flavors sharper, and it continues to evolve," Romina says. "That's why I think it's alive and magical."

Romina describes learning about how to make pisco as an oral history, something you can't learn from books alone. Eduardo taught her everything she needed to know to take over as head distiller. Part of her job is balancing tradition and culture, while bringing it into today's market. Traditionally in making pisco, women stomped on the grapes to extract the juice. Why women? Well, turns out they tend to weigh less than men and

were therefore less likely to crush the pits, which could make the pisco bitter. This process was time-consuming and labor-intensive, but the benefit was that the grapes were being macerated for a long time in their own juice, causing the skins to release phenols, the compounds responsible for the stunning aromatics present in pisco. Romina reintroduced this maceration step, but with the use of the bladder press, a technological advance in wine-making. She did her own research while consulting with Eduardo on the changes. "I'm always going back to him to check in, like, 'Hey, are the phenols being extracted when you're stomping on the grapes?'" she says. "And he's like, 'Yeah of course, why are you asking me that?'"

In addition to being CEO and head distiller of Capurro, Romina founded the Craft Spirits Cooperative in 2012. "When Capurro got to the States, we were a small family company without a giant budget. There was no platform that would help me build or distribute my brand the way I wanted," she says, so Romina started one herself. The Craft Spirits Cooperative now represents artisanal spirits from around the world, with the goal to bring more producers like her grandfather to the forefront of the industry.

Romina is a true hustler. She has a sharp eye for business, but approaches everything she does with an open heart. She uses her unique perspective being both American and Peruvian to create opportunities for other small business owners. "I'm at a very interesting intersection. I was raised Peruvian in the States, I speak both languages. I can manage and live in both worlds, and not everybody has that," Romina says. "I want to be that bridge."

# GOLDEN HOUR

Romina has fond memories of sitting outside with her family in Peru, eating lunch and drinking pisco before taking a siesta. But in her regular day-to-day life, she's a busy woman with a family who's running two full-time companies. This cocktail takes a no-frills approach to drink-making, while still evoking the feeling of a leisurely outdoor meal with loved ones. Capurro pisco is fragrant and vegetal, a perfect playmate for fresh produce and herbs. Cucumber and basil bring a straight-from-the-garden vibe, while the poblano liqueur accents the peppery notes in the pisco. And a pour-and-go cocktail is perfect for someone who has so many irons in the fire like Romina does. If you've only ever had pisco in its eponymous cocktail, the Pisco Sour, this drink is another easy and accessible way to enjoy this delicious spirit.

Makes 1 drink

4 cucumber slices, about ½ inch thick

4 basil leaves

¼ ounce simple syrup (page 218)

2 ounces Capurro pisco

¾ ounce fresh lime juice

½ ounce Ancho Reyes Verde poblano liqueur

Gently muddle the cucumber and basil with simple syrup in the bottom of a shaker tin. Add the pisco, lime juice, and poblano liqueur and fill with ice. Shake until chilled, then pour into a rocks glass and serve.

**LOLA PEDRO**

"To anyone that fancies themselves an alcohol connoisseur, I can say, 'Name me one indigenous African spirit,' and they can't," says Lola Pedro. "It's an extremely diverse continent of over a billion people, and we haven't unlocked a single indigenous spirit from there? That, for me, is a big shame." A born and bred Londoner of Nigerian heritage, Lola wanted to change this perception and bring òógóró, a native West African palm spirit, to the global market. In 2017, the entrepreneur and her business partner, Chibu Akukwe, launched Pedro's, Nigeria's first premium craft liquor brand, spearheading a movement to give African spirits their rightful due.

In 2013, Lola relocated from London to Lagos, Nigeria, "to basically find my roots." She traveled around the country, and as someone who enjoys a good drink, she was always on the hunt for regional spirits. But she found that people were mainly drinking imported products, usually the same handful of international spirits brands. "Any time I would ask the dreaded question, 'What have you got that's local?' Everyone would get quite nervous and say, 'No, you don't talk about that,'" she recalls. Lola was traveling through Nigeria's Delta State, and found herself in

the village of Sapele, when she joined a group of men sitting under a tree, drinking ògógóró. "That night, I was sold," she says. "The flavor profiles are so unique; it's a clear spirit that is ridiculously complex. I was absolutely fascinated." When she got back to Lagos, she learned about ògógóró's reputation as a dodgy, unregulated spirit, often called "illicit gin." This didn't make sense with what she had tasted in Sapele, so Lola embarked on a journey to discover the truth about ògógóró, reclaim the spirit, and restore its legacy. "The idea was, can we take something that's indigenous, illegal, and ostracized and distill it in

a way that meets global standards?" she says. "Can we convince people that this spirit is something that they can and should drink?"

Ògógóró is made from the sap of the raffia palm tree. Considered sacred in West Africa, the palm tree is used for nearly everything: Soap and furniture are made from it; the husks are used as fuel; it can be made into woven baskets and used to roof houses. First, the palm sap ferments and becomes palm wine, which is then distilled into a clear spirit called ògógóró. It dates back several centuries and is deeply entrenched in the social fabric of West Africa, where it is often used for traditional ceremonies like weddings and funerals.

When the British colonized Nigeria in the late nineteenth century, they decided to make this beautiful native spirit illegal to prevent the local communities from profiting off it. The British wanted to sell their own liquor, mainly gin, so they labeled òg̣óg̣óró as dirty, dangerous, and low-class (hence the incorrect nickname "illicit gin"). Like moonshine during America's Prohibition era, distilling òg̣óg̣óró had to become secretive. Because of that, the spirit actually became what the British said it was: unsafe. It was an underground product that was fairly dangerous to consume, and something that Nigerians did not have pride in. Lola wanted to bring òg̣óg̣óró out of the shadows, produce it safely, and return it to its former glory.

To make Pedro's, Lola and Chibu get òg̣óg̣óró from various villages in rural Nigeria, then bring it back to Lagos to redistill and package it. "We don't want to cut people out of the supply chain and gentrify òg̣óg̣óró," Lola explains. "We want to create the best product we can with the skill set that currently exists." Over the course of a year, Lola dedicated herself to learning all about òg̣óg̣óró. She spent weeks at a time in the rural countryside, cooking and distilling the clear spirit, and learning the fundamentals of its production. It wasn't easy to earn the villagers' trust, however. ("Not only was it strange that we wanted to make it premium, but I'm a woman with a British accent," she says.) Lola ended up befriending a local enforcer named T, who acted as her guide through the forest.

In the Yorùbáland villages with which Lola primarily works, only women are allowed to distill òg̣óg̣óró, a contrast from most other states where men oversee production. "The women make the òg̣óg̣óró for the village fresh in the morning, the way you'd have a coffee. They distill as they're cooking," she says. Stills are made from industrial oil drums, relics from when the Niger Delta was an oil-rich region. As an homage to this, the Pedro's bottle is a scaled-down dimension of an oil drum, and their signature crest has symbols of important aspects of ògógóró production: the palm, the fire, the drums, the machete, the water, and the people. On the side of the bottle embossed in copper is a powerful manifesto, starting with "I am not illegal" and ending with "I am ours." Pedro's is Africa's first premium ògógóró brand, and the first to ever be sold outside the continent.

To the villagers, what Lola and Chibu are doing is outrageous. "People still laugh. They think this is a joke or a weird dream," she says. But Lola's determination in making ògógóró an upscale product and introducing it to a larger audience has huge benefits; not just for African spirits writ large, but for the villagers themselves. "A lot of women that we work with use that money to put their kids through school," explains Lola. "That for me is where it stops being funny and it starts becoming a little bit profound. It's genuinely making a difference."

Taste-wise, Pedro's ògógóró could be compared to a rhum agricole or a soft tequila, but it really is unique unto itself with three distinct flavor profiles: citrus, spice, and creaminess. Lola and Chibu first distributed Pedro's to some of the most high-end spots in Lagos, and it quickly garnered attention and acclaim. Pedro's now has distribution in several African countries, as well as international markets, with goals to hit every major global city.

Lola has always been someone who marches to the beat of her own oil drum. With Pedro's, she's forging the path for the whole of Africa to celebrate their regional spirits. "We're spreading this gospel to consumers, people in the industry and other markets to find your indigenous spirit and get it in a bottle," says Lola. "Let's distill it, let's make it proper, and let's enjoy it."

# I AM OURS

Because òǵógóró is probably new to those outside West Africa, I felt it was important to let the spirit shine and not get swallowed up by big flavors. Lola loves using òǵógóró in egg sour cocktails because "it still celebrates those citrus notes, and the egg white gives a velvety texture that is fantastic with òǵógóró, because it's the mouthfeel of the spirit as well." Banana liqueur provides a soft flavor that pairs excellently with òǵógóró, and nutmeg gives the cocktail a delicious aromatic note. It's as luxurious and upscale as Lola has made Pedro's òǵógóró.

Makes 1 drink

1 ½ ounces Pedro's òǵógóró

¾ ounce banana liqueur

½ ounce fresh lime juice

¼ ounce simple syrup (page 218)

1 large egg white

1 banana leaf, for garnish

Freshly grated nutmeg, for garnish

Combine the òǵógóró, banana liqueur, lime juice, simple syrup, and egg white in a shaker tin. Dry shake (see page 15), then add ice and shake again until chilled. Double strain into a coupe, garnish with the banana leaf and nutmeg, and serve.

FOUNDER OF
KASAMA
RUM

# ALEXANDRA DORDA

**A**lexandra Dorda grew up in the spirits business. When she was a child, her Polish father cofounded two luxury vodka brands, Belvedere and Chopin, and nearly every day felt like bring-your-daughter-to-work day. "I remember being as young as five years old, and every time we would go to a restaurant, my dad would always say, 'Alex, we have to see if we have distribution here. We have to see what's on the cocktail menu,'" she recalls. With a mother from the Philippines (one of the largest rum-producing countries in the world), it's no surprise that Alexandra wanted to combine her alcohol industry acumen with her pride for her Filipino heritage, and in 2020, she founded her own spirits brand, Kasama Rum.

Vodka might have been the liquor that got all the attention in her family, but Alexandra decided to take a different path. She came to the idea of Kasama first as a consumer, taking issue with how the rum category was marketed. "So much of rum has been stuck in a rut of pirates and sailors. It's very nautical and antiquated," she says. "There are lots of fantastic rums, but nobody was talking about rum in a modern and fresh way." Alexandra wanted to create a new rum brand that was approachable from both a price point and flavor

profile, and one that would appeal to consumers like her. "I saw that I could fill that gap with something that was a beautiful spirit but was also a vehicle to tell the story about my Filipino culture."

Alexandra's company is as global as she is. She starts by sourcing rum in the Philippines, where it's distilled from fresh-pressed sugarcane juice and aged in American oak barrels. Next, it's brought to the Dorda family distillery in Poland where it is blended, bottled, and packaged. Kasama is distributed all over the world, with the United States as its main market. The rum is bold and fruit-forward, with flavors of banana, pineapple, and vanilla. "I wanted it to be something that was good for sipping on its own, but also a good base for cocktails," she says.

Kasama means "together" in Filipino and embodies the message Alexandra wants to share. "What I love most about the alcohol industry at large is that, at its very best, it really does bring people together. It's a way that people celebrate important

milestones or connect with others," says Alexandra. "The Philippines has a very friendly, warm, and convivial culture, so it spoke to that ethos as well."

Alexandra wants to help change the perception of rum, much like her dad did with vodka in the nineties. "I hope that someone will look at Kasama in the future and say, 'there's this whole new appreciation for rum, and it started, among others, with this brand,'" she says. Embodying the meaning of her company's name, Alexandra has partnered with other Filipino entrepreneurs. She collaborated with Filipino American designer Josie Natori on a limited-edition bottle to raise money for Voice of the Free, a Manila-based charity that works to end modern-day slavery. She's done events with Filipino restaurants, worked with Filipino makeup brands, and created food products with other Filipino-run companies. "The best part about launching Kasama is finding other people who have pride in our culture and who are excited to amplify that in creative ways," she says. "It's just been such a blessing."

# JET-SETTER

Alexandra loves going against the stereotype of super-sweet, tropical rum libations and drinking Kasama in savory cocktails, so I created an old-fashioned variation using two quintessential Filipino ingredients: tamarind and chiles. Tamarind syrup gives a beautiful earthy and slightly sour note, while the poblano liqueur provides a gentle spice, balancing out Kasama's strong fruit flavors. Finally, a fresh lime twist gives the cocktail a bright zing. (Careful not to leave the twist in the drink for too long, though, as the pith of lime peels can be very bitter.) This is an adventurous and worldly old-fashioned to enjoy with your friends and family—even if they're vodka people.

Makes 1 drink

2 ounces Kasama Rum

½ ounce Tamarind Syrup (recipe follows)

¼ ounce Ancho Reyes Verde poblano liqueur

1 lime twist, for garnish

Combine the rum, tamarind syrup, and poblano liqueur in a rocks glass over a big ice cube and stir until chilled. Garnish with the lime twist and serve.

## TAMARIND SYRUP
Makes about ⅔ cup

½ cup Demerara sugar

2 teaspoons tamarind paste concentrate

In a small saucepan, combine ½ cup water, the sugar, and the tamarind paste. Heat over medium heat, stirring, until the sugar and tamarind have dissolved, about 5 minutes. Remove from the heat and let cool. Transfer to a nonreactive airtight container and cover. Store in the fridge for up to 1 week.

COFOUNDER
OF
ARAK FARID

JESS KANDALAFT

**A**bout an hour outside of Beirut, Jess Kandalaft and her husband, Fred Abi Khalil, distill a traditional Lebanese spirit for a new generation. Nestled in the cedar forests with a view of the Mediterranean Sea, Jess and Fred make arak, a grape- and aniseed-based liquor common in the Levantine region of the Middle East. Inspired by Fred's family's affinity for arak and using Jess's modern design sensibility, the couple have created a new brand meant to shine a light on this magnificent spirit.

It's very common for people to make their own arak in the villages of Lebanon. Nearly every household has a pot still, and arak is traditionally made by the elders. "We liked the process a lot. The smell of the arak when it's being made, the gathering around the pot still," explains Jess. "So we said, 'Why don't we learn how to make it?'" In 2017, the couple cobbled together various arak recipes, and eventually settled on their own, sharing it with friends and family. Their hobby soon turned profitable: one friend loved their arak so much, he bought all seven of their homemade gallons. It was the start of their new spirits brand, Arak Farid, named in honor of Fred's late grandfather Farid.

Both born and raised in Lebanon, Jess and Fred met as teenagers at a mall in Beirut, and bonded over their shared love of metal music. ("Fred gave me his earphones from his iPod Nano and said, 'Do you want to listen to some music?'" Jess recalls.) While they're still city-dwellers, they chose to distill arak in the small village of Ain Jouaiya, where Fred would spend summers with his grandparents. "It was very primitive at first," says Jess. They started production outside the family house, often distilling in the rain, with Fred's father shielding them with a big umbrella. Eventually, they fixed up a little room that now functions as the distillery, and they officially launched Arak Farid in 2019. "It's still very small, but at least there's a roof," Jess says.

Arak is the national drink of Lebanon, often mixed with water or ice. It's one of the oldest spirits in the world—production of arak can be dated back to the ninth century. A special feature of arak (and other anise-based spirits) is that it instantly turns milky white when combined with water, like a magic trick. Arak Farid is distinctly anise-forward, with notes of fennel, licorice, and green pepper. At 54% ABV, it packs a punch while being soft and warming at the same time.

With her background as a graphic designer, Jess designed all the branding for Arak Farid. To Lebanon's younger generations, arak is considered old-school. "I wanted to break that image and modernize it," she says. Jess chose to have the label feature Farid's face over a manifesto of sorts—it's a striking illustration, and certainly attracts attention. "We created this tribute to him, and I wanted to have his image speak to you on the bottle." The other design elements also feel streamlined and contemporary, using a calming, royal blue motif.

The longtime couple have faced many challenges together, both as business owners and as Lebanese citizens. There are electricity issues throughout the country, interrupting the distillation process. "We've gone many hours during the day without electricity, and it was really challenging for us to work," Jess says. As if living through a national economic crisis and a global pandemic weren't enough, the couple also resided near the Port of Beirut when the explosion occurred there in 2020; their house was partially destroyed in the blast.

Jess and Fred thought about leaving their home country, as many of their friends have, but ultimately decided to stay. "We didn't want to focus on what's going to set us back," says Jess. She wholeheartedly believes in their mission to bring arak to a wider, contemporary audience, while simultaneously honoring a beloved relative. That's enough to keep going, even when times get tough. "We created something that we don't want to lose, and this is why we've been trying to continue ever since."

# FRESH MIST

Arak is traditionally sipped on its own, but it's being featured more frequently in mixed drinks as cocktail culture has grown around the world. Arak Farid is personality-driven and heavy on the anise flavor, so the key is to pair it with other ingredients that can stand up to it. Inviting crème de cassis (black currant liqueur) and rosemary to the party is a way of embracing arak's savory notes. Pineapple juice harnesses the inherent sweetness in arak and echoes the round mouthfeel. Adding seltzer mellows everything out, while nodding to the ritual of mixing arak with water. Juicy, full-flavored, bold—this cocktail is a fresh and fun take on how to drink arak, and hopefully supports Jess's quest to bring arak into the modern-day spirits industry.

Makes 1 drink

1 ounce Arak Farid

¾ ounce pineapple juice

½ ounce fresh lemon juice

½ ounce crème de cassis

¼ ounce simple syrup (page 218)

Seltzer, to top

1 rosemary sprig, for garnish

Combine the arak, pineapple juice, lemon juice, crème de cassis, and simple syrup in a shaker tin with a few ice cubes. Shake until chilled, then strain into an ice-filled Collins glass and top with seltzer. Garnish with the rosemary sprig and serve.

T he Nonino family has been in the distilling business since 1897. In the small region of Friuli, Italy, they've made groundbreaking contributions to the spirits industry over six generations, including revolutionizing the way grappa is made and creating an amaro that is now essential in the craft cocktail world. What's perhaps more remarkable is that women in the Nonino family have been in charge of the company since 1940, a time when Italian women didn't yet have the right to vote. Today, three generations of Nonino women are continuing their family legacy and taking the distillery to new heights. They are boisterous and vibrant, overflowing with passion and love for each other and what they do.

Let's start with some brief family history: Antonio Nonino, the third generation of Noninos, married Silvia in 1928, and they made grappa and a variety of liqueurs. When Antonio died in World War II, Silvia took over the company, becoming Italy's first female master distiller. Silvia and Antonio's son, Benito, married Giannola in 1962 and together, the couple set out to change the method of making grappa throughout the country. Giannola and Benito had three daughters, Cristina, Elisabetta, and Antonella, who continued to grow

189

the Nonino legacy. Cristina's daughter Francesca is the sixth generation of "this crazy family of distillers" (as she calls them), and is now introducing grappa to a whole new demographic. Brava!

Grappa is an Italian grape-based brandy made by distilling pomace, the seeds, stalks, and stems that are left over after pressing grapes for wine-making. Italians have been distilling grappa for centuries, and it was long considered a peasant spirit, a regional drink of locals. The grappa industry has grown immensely, but while popular, grappa developed a reputation of being poor quality, given away to tourists at the end of a meal. And a lot of it *is* of poor quality, made with cheap, industrial ingredients (industrial distillers make around 80 percent of the grappa sold in Italy). When made honorably, grappa is a delicious representation of the beauty of Italy. Nonino is an artisanal distillery that makes and bottles all their own products, a rarity in the industry.

This grappa revolution started with Giannola and Benito, who transformed the perception of grappa from a ubiquitously mediocre, poor man's spirit into an exquisite product that is emblematic of Italy. "My grandma and grandpa worked to prove to people that grappa was not this fire water, but could be something beautiful and elegant," Francesca says. In 1973, Giannola and Benito started

distilling pomace from a single grape varietal, rather than a mix of winery leftovers, something that had never been done in the grappa industry. Giannola and Benito created the first single-varietal, premium grappa, and soon other producers began copying their methods. "We were able to transform grappa from what was considered the Cinderella of spirits into the queen of them," says Giannola. "It's magical!" Giannola has been rightly recognized for her work: In 1998, she was named a Cavaliere del Lavoro by the Italian president, recognizing her contributions to the world of business (she is also one of only twenty-five women to receive the prize); she was given a special honorary degree in business economics by the University of Udine; and in 2009, she was awarded the International Eva Prize, naming her Entrepreneur of the Year.

While Giannola and Benito focused on distilling grappa, their daughters turned their attention to the liqueurs, reviving their grandfather's original amaro recipe. Amaro is an herbaceous, bittersweet Italian liqueur, traditionally consumed as an after-dinner drink. In 1992, the sisters tweaked their grandfather's formula and developed Amaro Nonino Quintessentia. It's citrusy and herbal with notes of chocolate and is undoubtedly Nonino's best-selling product, now a staple in cocktail bars all over the world.

When you enter a family business that's been going for over a hundred years, you don't exactly apply for a specific job. "We don't have a CEO or board members," Elisabetta explains. "We have family members, and everybody needs to work." Cristina is in charge of Italy and Switzerland (she's not a fan of flying); Antonella is the liaison for Germany and Austria; Elisabetta takes care of North America; and matriarch Giannola oversees the whole operation. After working within various areas of the business, Francesca

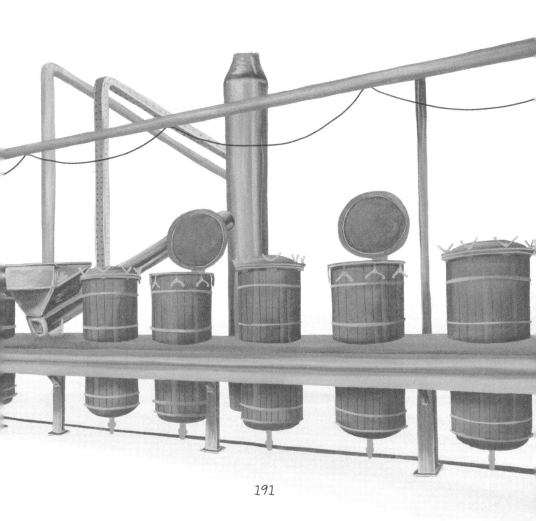

exercised her grandchild privilege: "We have a saying in Italian, 'The parsley goes everywhere.' At a certain point I went to my family and said, 'Guys, I cannot be the parsley anymore, please give me a specific market.'" So Elisabetta whisked Francesca away to the United States on her next trip, and now they work together on North American sales.

In 2018, the Nonino women resurrected another family liqueur: Grandma Silvia's apéritif from 1940. The original apéritif was called Aperitivo Bianco, and Cristina studied the recipe for years, wanting to keep the natural essence of Silvia's recipe. She decided to incorporate gentian root and rhubarb for a slightly bitter note, resulting in L'Aperitivo Nonino. It's all-natural, made from eighteen different botanicals and distilled from the pomace of Fragolino grapes, a strawberry grape that tastes like wild berries. This apéritif is a liquid representation of the history of the Nonino women: The label symbolizes the four generations of women, all holding glasses as if they're drinking with you. When Giannola can't sleep, she makes herself a nightcap of L'Aperitivo Nonino, a couple of lemon slices, tonic water, and ice. "After that, I'm able to go to sleep happily," she says.

As a millennial, Francesca is also the distillery's web communications manager. She's built a robust online presence educating people about grappa. As "the grappa influencer," she feels it's important to share the story of the Nonino company and family with a wider audience. Francesca has goals of eventually becoming Nonino's master distiller. "The master distiller takes the soul or the essence of the raw material and puts it in the final glass," she says. "I think there isn't anything more beautiful than that." The Nonino distillery is arguably as strong and successful as it ever was. Nonino's grappas and liqueurs have won countless awards, as has the distillery itself, including being named "Best Distillery in the World" in 2019 by *Wine Enthusiast*.

The Nonino women are feisty and driven, and they are immensely proud of their generational heritage. Every family member is continuing the mission set by their ancestors, to share their story and passion. "When you do something with your name, the name of your family, you want to protect that," says Francesca. "To be able to do that means to never accept anything less than the best."

# LE DONNE

There's perhaps nothing more Italian than enjoying an afternoon spritz, and this cocktail honoring the Nonino women fits the bill. The base of the drink is bittersweet L'Aperitivo Nonino, with notes of elderflower, rhubarb, and citrus. Amaro Nonino is a natural pairing, thanks to its bright herbaceousness, and gives the cocktail a bit of depth. Rose syrup brings a delicate floral quality (spray a bit of rose water over the top for extra rosiness), and, of course, both seltzer and Prosecco are employed for their ever-important bubbles. This is a delightfully refreshing and aromatic drink to enjoy with all the women in your life. Saluti!

Makes 1 drink

1 ¼ ounces L'Aperitivo Nonino

¾ ounce Amaro Nonino

½ ounce fresh lemon juice

¼ ounce Rose Syrup (recipe follows)

1 ounce seltzer

Prosecco, to top

1 lemon twist, for garnish

Rose water in an atomizer, for garnish

Combine the aperitivo, amaro, lemon juice, rose syrup, and seltzer in an ice-filled wineglass and stir gently. Top with the Prosecco, garnish with the lemon twist and a spritz of rose water, and serve.

## ROSE SYRUP
### Makes about 1 ½ cups

1 cup sugar

½ cup food-grade dried rosebuds

In a small saucepan, combine 1 cup water and the sugar and bring to a simmer over low heat, stirring until the sugar fully dissolves. Remove from the heat, then stir in the rosebuds and steep for 20 minutes. Fine strain into a nonreactive airtight container and let cool. Cover and store in the refrigerator for up to 2 weeks.

**N**itzan Podoswa Marrun is a geographer of spirits. As the cofounder of Cardenxe Sotol, she is dedicated to introducing people to a Mexican spirit that isn't named "tequila" or "mezcal." With thirty-two states, sixty-eight indigenous languages, and multiple types of climates, of course a country as vast as Mexico makes more than two styles of alcohol. "There's an infinite world of possibilities when it comes to Mexico and distilled spirits," she says.

Born in Mexico City, Nitzan grew up in a tequila-drinking family, as her grandmother had a connection to someone in tequila production who made her a personalized batch of the agave spirit every year. Soon, Nitzan "completely fell in love with the whole Mexican distilled spirits industry." At the end of 2020, she got a call from a high school friend, Luigi Ambrosi, who wanted to learn about indigenous Mexican music and suggested they go on a road trip. Nitzan proposed that they visit the home of Los Cardencheros de Sapioriz, a group that performs Canto Cardenche, a near-extinct musical genre native to northern Mexico. The two friends hit the road and drove from Durango City up to Sapioriz to meet the Cardencheros. Along the way, they kept encountering a regional spirit called sotol.

Sotol has been distilled in northern Mexico for over three centuries. Unlike tequila and mezcal, which are made from agave, sotol is made from the heart of the *Dasylirion* plant and can only be made in three Mexican states: Chihuahua, Durango, and Coahuila.

As for how it tastes: If tequila is straightforward and mezcal is nuanced, sotol lies somewhere in the middle. While it's often bright and grassy, it can also be earthy and vegetal.

When Nitzan and Luigi reached the Cardencheros, the band welcomed them with open arms. They learned that people often drank sotol before singing in order to open and prepare their throats. Canto Cardenche is a beautiful and harrowing genre of music; it's sung a capella, centered on themes of love and sorrow, and has been passed down through generations in rural Mexico. Sipping on sotol while listening to the Cardencheros, both Nitzan and Luigi became enamored with the region and its spirit. When they went to Chihuahua, they found that sotol there tasted wildly different from the spirit they'd had in Durango. "It's crazy how something from the same plant can taste so different just because of where it's growing," Nitzan says. "The terroir really affects the flavor." They named their brand Cardenxe (pronounced car-DEN-che) in honor of the Cardencheros, and officially launched in 2022.

Cardenxe works with three separate distilleries in different landscapes and honors the traditional distilling methods of each region. "The idea was we would respect what the master distiller wanted, but also respect the terroir as much as possible," Nitzan says. The Sotol de Desierto is made in Coyame, in central Chihuahua; it's dry, almost sandy, and a little floral. The Sotol de la Sierra is made in the Chihuahuan woods of Ciudad Madera and is mossy and piney. And the Sotol de Pradera comes from the prairie of Nombre de Dios in Durango and has notes of toasted corn.

One of the biggest roadblocks Cardenxe faces is that they're a brand-new spirit category to those outside Mexico, but a huge difference between sotol and agave spirits is the sustainability factor. *Dasylirion* plant harvesting is controlled and limited by a regulatory body, a lesson learned from the tequila and mezcal industry's overharvesting of wild agave. "Once you learn a little bit about the industry, I think you start becoming a little more responsible when you drink," Nitzan says.

With Cardenxe, Nitzan is on a mission to bring awareness to this ancient Mexican spirit and celebrate both sotol's rich history and the expansive culture of her home country. "Every time we head towards the distilleries, there's a new adventure. We meet some new people, we learn something new about the culture." It may not be tequila, but Nitzan is certainly following in her grandmother's footsteps with her hyperlocal, highly delicious sotol.

# UN AMOR PENDIENTE

This cocktail is named after the Los Cardencheros de Sapioriz album of the same title, meaning "a pending love." Fitting, as Nitzan is determined to have everyone soon fall in love with sotol. It's a great way to introduce the spirit to a new audience. Nitzan is a huge fan of fresh produce in cocktails, so I reached for tomatillos, a fruit native to Mexico and Central America. Charring the tomatillos before juicing adds a subtle smokiness, and is a great pairing with herbaceous cilantro (apologies to all the cilantro haters out there). All the ingredients play off the earthy and floral notes present in the Sotol de Desierto, making a bright and savory margarita variation that feels of the land, perfect for quenching your thirst before bursting into song.

Makes 1 drink

Handful of cilantro leaves, plus 1 cilantro sprig for garnish

¾ ounce simple syrup (page 218)

1 ½ ounces Cardenxe Sotol de Desierto

¾ ounce Charred Tomatillo Juice (recipe follows)

½ ounce fresh lime juice

3 drops saline solution (page 217)

Gently muddle the cilantro leaves and simple syrup in the bottom of a shaker tin. Add the sotol, tomatillo juice, lime juice, and saline solution and shake with ice. Double strain into a rocks glass over ice. Garnish with the cilantro sprig and serve.

## CHARRED TOMATILLO JUICE
Makes about ½ cup

1 pound tomatillos (8 to 10 medium), husked

Heat a grill pan or a cast-iron skillet on the stovetop over medium-high heat. Add the tomatillos and grill on both sides until the skins have bubbled and blackened, about 8 minutes. (You can also do this under your oven's broiler; just be sure to remove the tomatillos after 5 to 7 minutes, before they pop.) Juice the tomatillos, then fine strain into a nonreactive airtight container and cover. Store in the refrigerator for up to 4 days.

COFOUNDER
OF AVALLEN
CALVADOS

STEPHANIE JORDAN

tephanie Jordan has a deep love of the land. Raised in the rolling hills of Beaujolais in France, she first thought she wanted to get into the wine business. "I wanted to save the Beaujolais! Now, the Beaujolais doesn't need saving anymore, but it did in 2005," she says. She indeed started her career in wine, then moved to spirits when she joined the sales team of Diageo, where she primarily was the global brand ambassador for Tanqueray gin. Working for an international spirits company made her think about the importance of drinking local and more biodiverse products. "I could almost guarantee that

if I went to a top tier bar anywhere in the world, they'd all have Tanqueray. I could drink a Tanqueray martini wherever I went," Stephanie says. "And I thought, how sad is that? The way we currently sell and promote spirits is hugely unsustainable."

After nine years at Diageo, Stephanie and her coworker Tim Etherington-Judge decided to start their own liquor company. They set out to make the most sustainable spirit possible by looking at four key categories: water, biodiversity loss, pesticide use, and carbon emissions. All of their research pointed to one raw ingredient: "apples, apples, apples, apples and apples from the orchards of Normandy. Avallen was born as an accidental calvados."

Calvados is apple brandy made in Normandy, France, and it's not exactly en vogue. Most calvados are in dark, squat bottles, often gathering dust on liquor store shelves. Avallen, which means "apple tree" in old Cornish, stands out; it's sleek and colorful, made to be enjoyed in mixed drinks rather than sipped as a digestif. It tastes fresh and vibrant, and is uniquely apple-forward. "By no means is this a traditional heritage calvados. This is a sustainably focused spirits brand, which happens to be a calvados," says Stephanie. "It's about trying to bring back a product that focuses on the fruit." Avallen is distilled from forty different varieties of apples, all pesticide free. "Our apples are not super big, cute, and shiny," she says. "They're tiny, funny shapes, they're all beat up, they're all colors, and they're nonedible varietals, so making calvados is really what they're destined to do."

Stephanie is passionate, caring wholeheartedly about the environment and her work. She looks at sustainability from a holistic perspective, taking every step of the process into account. That starts with using less water—a single bottle of Avallen requires only 1 liter of water from field to bottle. A cornerstone of the company is giving back to organizations to help protect wild bees, which pollinate Normandy apples. "Every single blossom that became a French apple that went into Avallen was pollinated by a wild bee," Stephanie explains. "Without the bees, there are no apples." Stephanie and Tim are also focused on making their packaging eco-friendly, trying to remove the need for single-use glass by launching a paper bottle and refillable kegs.

Stephanie believes the spirits industry has immense power in propelling the sustainability movement, because what we drink tells a story. "We should be talking about biodiversity, raw material, drinking fruit. The way we've built society is through the stories we tell. If we can see it, we can do it. It's hard, but it's about getting that energy and positivity behind the movement," says Stephanie. "It makes me excited."

# APPLES, APPLES, APPLES

For Stephanie, I wanted to make a cocktail that was entirely zero-waste. This riff on a Manhattan (the Big Apple!) utilizes apples in a few different ways, starting with poaching apples in sweet vermouth, then using the skins, cores, and seeds to make apple honey. (Honey, of course, is a nod to the bees.) The result is rich, fruity, and fragrant. And as a bonus, you can eat those poached apples with ice cream for dessert!

Makes 1 drink

2 ounces Avallen calvados

1 ounce Poached Apple Vermouth (recipe follows)

1 barspoon Apple Honey (recipe follows)

4 dashes Angostura bitters

Combine all the ingredients in a mixing glass filled with ice and stir until chilled. Strain into a Nick and Nora glass and serve.

## POACHED APPLE VERMOUTH AND APPLE HONEY
Makes about 1½ cups vermouth and 1 cup honey

2 medium apples (go for something on the mildly sweet side, like Gala), peeled, quartered, and cored (skin and cores reserved)

2 cups Italian sweet vermouth, preferably Carpano Antica

½ cup honey

In a large saucepan, combine the apples and vermouth. Cover loosely with parchment paper and bring to a simmer over medium-low heat. Simmer, turning the apples occasionally so they poach evenly, until the apples are fork-tender, 20 to 25 minutes. Meanwhile, in a small saucepan, combine the honey and ½ cup water and bring to a simmer over low heat. Stir in the reserved apple skin and cores and simmer, stirring occasionally, for 10 minutes. Remove from the heat and let cool for 20 minutes, then fine strain into a nonreactive airtight container and cover. Store in the refrigerator for up to 2 weeks.

Carefully remove the apples from the vermouth (discard them or save them to eat with ice cream for dessert), then fine strain the vermouth into a nonreactive airtight container and let cool. Cover and store in the refrigerator for up to 1 month.

**EFFIE PANAGOPOULOS**

Effie Panagopoulos was at a beach bar in Mykonos in 2008 when she had an epiphany. All around her, American tourists were doing shots of a Greek liqueur called mastiha (*mahs-TEE-ha*), so she took one too. "I had this Proustian rush when I first tasted mastiha in an alcohol form, bringing me back to being five years old in the village with my grandmother," she recalls. Inspired by the wild success of St-Germain, an elderflower liqueur that had launched a year prior, she decided she wanted to bring mastiha to the United States. "The taste, my grandmother, St-Germain, like it was all in that one moment, that lightbulb," she says. "I'm going to fucking do this."

Born and raised in Boston to Greek immigrant parents, Effie initially had goals of being a UN ambassador. After tending bar to get through college, she taught high school Spanish during the day and moonlit as a rep for Midori melon liqueur, her first foray into spirits. After a stint at Bacardi Limited, she became the national brand ambassador for Metaxa, a Greek brandy. ("My mother was like, 'Hmm, at least you're finally the ambassador of something.'") Effie's job with Metaxa is what brought her to that aha moment in Mykonos, and ultimately led her to founding her company, Kleos.

The Greeks have been distilling mastiha for over three thousand years. The raw ingredient of the same name is a sap that comes from the mastic tree, a small evergreen indigenous to the Greek island of Chios. This sap has a myriad of healing properties, including being used for digestive issues and dental hygiene. In fact, mastiha was the world's first chewing gum. (Not to sound like the dad in *My Big Fat Greek Wedding*, but the word "masticate" comes from the Greek word *mastika*, meaning "to chew.") As an alcohol, mastiha is often thought of as a peasant spirit and before Kleos, it had never been mass-marketed outside of Greece. A lot of mastiha brands are cheap and made of artificial flavors; like grappa in Italy, mastiha developed a bad reputation that Effie is seeking to change. "I want Kleos to be the standard of mastiha," she says.

It took Effie a full decade to get Kleos off the ground. She did seventeen different formulas and worked with several distilleries until she locked in on the right liquid. "There was no way that I was going to put out a product to market that wasn't as perfect as it could be," she says. Effie ended up choosing a recipe made by Maroussa Tsachaki, a female distiller in Greece with a PhD in flavor science. "We did six formulas with her, and she had no ego at all. The male distiller I worked with, he wouldn't experiment," she recalls. "With Maroussa, she was like, 'I'm going to nail this for you.'"

Kleos mastiha is a chameleon. It has hints of cucumber, mint, and sweet tea, but also has earthy and vegetal notes. Unlike other liqueurs, it can be used as a base spirit because it's significantly lower in sugar (Kleos only has 2 grams of sugar per ounce, whereas other liqueurs can contain nearly five times that much). It can be consumed by itself on the rocks or with a squeeze of lemon, but it's great in mixed drinks as well. Effie chose the name Kleos because the word in Greek can be translated to "eternal glory." "I'm trying to bring the glory back to Greek spirits and make us relevant on the back bar again," says Effie. "It's funny because now I truly do feel like an ambassador to Greece."

Effie has built Kleos from the ground up, often as a one-woman show. "It's been a grueling road. I slept on my mom's couch to get the brand off in Boston. I raised just enough money to do a small production run," she says. "We're growing really fast, but I've never had enough working capital to meet the demand that existed." Effie believes that running out of money is typically what prevents most women-owned brands from getting to the next level.

Effie is impassioned and tenacious, using Kleos to highlight the beauty of Greece, as well as the power of other female entrepreneurs. "I'm more determined at this point to really change the narrative, to be able to invest in other woman-owned brands," she says. There's no doubt that Greece and mastiha are lucky to have someone as dedicated as Effie as their champion. "I will make this happen. From my mouth to God's ears, it's going to happen."

# THE AMBASSADOR

Ever the diplomat, Kleos is adaptable. It's not just another herbaceous liqueur—it's layered and complex, which makes it an exciting and fun ingredient. I wanted to create a cocktail that you could drink at a beach bar in Mykonos, but one that still tells a global story, much like Effie. Pomegranate and lemon juices bring the fruity, refreshing vibes, with pomegranate being a quintessential Greek ingredient. Effie loves pairing Kleos with agave spirits, so I added a touch of blanco tequila, which plays off the grassy quality in the liqueur. Seltzer lightens everything up, and a sprig of dill brings in Kleos's herby quality. The cocktail is bright and tart, sweet and luscious, and hopefully brings a little bit of glory.

Makes 1 drink

1 ½ ounces Kleos mastiha

¾ ounce pomegranate juice

¾ ounce fresh lemon juice

½ ounce blanco tequila

¼ ounce agave syrup (page 216)

Seltzer, to top

1 dill sprig, for garnish

Combine the mastiha, pomegranate juice, lemon juice, tequila, and agave syrup in a shaker tin filled with ice. Shake until chilled, then strain into an ice-filled Collins glass. Top with seltzer, garnish with the dill sprig, and serve.

# BRIDGETTE TAYLOR

**W**hen Bridgette Taylor declared her college major in history with a focus on medieval witchcraft, she probably didn't think she'd end up starting a vodka brand. As an enthusiastic home bartender, Bridgette always enjoyed mixing up concoctions, but never thought that spirits would become her career. Little did she know, the universe had a different idea bubbling in her cauldron.

Bridgette was about to receive her business degree from Harvard Business School and start a job in management consulting when the COVID-19 pandemic put a hex on the world. Like many of us,

Bridgette suddenly found herself with a lot of time on her hands, so she devoted herself to home mixology. "What started as this casual interest grew into a coping-mechanism obsession," she recalls. Bridgette noticed that the whole category of vodka was lacking in innovation and super-premium options, instead repeatedly seeing the same handful of brands on liquor store shelves. "I thought it could be really fun to take some of that beautiful storytelling and craftsmanship that's so celebrated in other spirit categories and bring it to vodka," she says. She decided to go all in on her new passion and create a new vodka brand, one that spoke to her aesthetics and interests, but would also fill a gap in the market.

Bridgette combined her love of witchcraft and craft spirits into Harridan Vodka, which launched at the end of 2020. Her senior thesis in college was on the medieval witch trials, and she'd always been interested in historical witchcraft. "I had a morbid curiosity about the witch trials," she says. "It was mostly women who were persecuted because they didn't fit the mold of what the patriarchy wanted them to be." Subverting the expectations of a female-owned vodka, Bridgette bottled this dark, spooky, Victorian aesthetic, and gave it an undercurrent of feminism, without being stereotypically feminine. When looking for a name that fit her concept, she came across the word "harridan," meaning "belligerent woman." "I looked at how the word was historically used, which was usually disparaging," Bridgette explains. "It was a guy being like, 'Ugh, I married a harridan, my wife is so angry and cranky.' I was like, I love this."

Harridan Vodka is made from organic corn in upstate New York and defies vodka's notoriety as a neutral spirit. It's a vodka for people who like to taste their liquor; it's bold yet smooth, with notes of citrus and black pepper, and mixes excellently in cocktail potions. It's also overproof—most vodkas are 40% ABV, whereas Harridan is 44% ABV, an initial distillery mistake that Bridgette chose to embrace. "Female-targeted spirits tend to be low-ABV for 'the delicate female palate,'" she says. "Well, screw that. Our mascot is an angry old lady. We're going to be overproof like she would want." The bottle is also striking: it's made from upcycled glass, hand-dipped with a black wax top, and the label design evokes the intricate borders of medieval texts. Harridan has also launched a few spooky limited-edition releases like the Paranormal Reserve (each bottle comes with a bespoke wooden case that doubles as a Ouija board) and the Midsummer Reserve to honor the summer solstice.

A self-proclaimed harridan herself, Bridgette is chic, savvy, and a shrewd businesswoman. She's casting a spell on the spirits industry, proving with Harridan that vodka can be just as worthy to pour in your chalice as any quality whiskey or tequila. "We want to be that pioneer, showing that the luxury version of this product does exist and deserves to exist," she says.

# OLD HAG

This cocktail is a cross between a Corpse Reviver and a Last Word, one of Bridgette's favorite drinks. It's herbaceous, balanced, and bracingly refreshing. Here Harridan Vodka takes the place of gin, as it can hold up to the distinct herbal flavor of Yellow Chartreuse, a French liqueur made by Carthusian monks. (Only the monks know the secret recipe for Chartreuse, kind of reminiscent of witches brewing a mysterious potion.) Pear eau-de-vie softens and rounds out the cocktail, while honey brings an aromatic sweetness and holds everything together. Absinthe, another cryptic concoction made from herbs and spices, provides a sharp anise aroma, and the brandied cherry at the bottom is the final sweet send-off, making this cocktail the perfect witch's brew.

Makes 1 drink

Absinthe, to rinse the glass (see page 15)

1 ½ ounces Harridan Vodka

½ ounce fresh lemon juice

½ ounce Yellow Chartreuse

½ ounce pear eau-de-vie

¼ ounce honey syrup (page 216)

1 brandied cherry, for garnish

Rinse a coupe with absinthe. Combine the vodka, lemon juice, Chartreuse, eau-de-vie, and honey syrup in a shaker tin filled with ice. Shake until chilled, then double strain into the prepared glass. Drop the brandied cherry into the glass and serve.

**EILEEN WAYNER, ALEX SMITH & LOLA THOMAS**

**E**very July, the spirits community gathers in New Orleans for a weeklong conference hosted by the Tales of the Cocktail Foundation. What started in 2002 as a walking tour of historic Big Easy bars has since become the world's largest cocktail and spirits festival, shaping the future and growth of the industry writ large. And believe it or not, Tales of the Cocktail (often shortened to Tales) is completely run by a badass, all-female leadership team.

The Tales of the Cocktail Foundation is just over a dozen employees strong. At the head of the small-but-mighty team is Eileen Wayner. Originally from Maryland, Eileen came from the arts and culture sector, and was named CEO of the Foundation in 2020.

"What I think is unique about me is I am an outsider," says Eileen. "I'm here to listen and reflect back what the goals are, and to help implement those things." New Orleans is a central character in Tales's story. "In general, the city is such a hub for culture, for music, for expression," Eileen says. "It has such an important history and legacy in the way that we approach hospitality." Over twenty thousand people descend upon the French Quarter for Tales every year, making a huge economic impact on the city during the otherwise slow summer season. And having the keen eye and compassionate ear of Eileen at the helm means that that impact goes a long way.

Of course, a cocktail conference is going to be a fun time, and

Tales certainly is a party (let's be real, it's an absolute *blast*). But a pillar of the weeklong event is the education component. Lola Thomas is Tales's program director, overseeing all the educational seminars, of which there are around seventy held in just five days. The seminars cover spirits and business education, as well as themes that extend outside of the typical bar space. "Our seminars are a key indicator of where trends are going because industry members are submitting ideas," says Lola. She also runs the Beyond the Bar initiative—providing workshops on issues like substance abuse—and the philanthropy committee, which gives away over a hundred thousand dollars to organizations that serve specific hospitality communities. "We're looking at bartending as a holistic career." Lola is perfectly situated as the leader of these local and global initiatives: she worked for the Peace Corps in West Africa, has a master's degree in human rights, and lived in New Orleans for several years before relocating to her home state of California.

Born and raised in Louisiana, Alex Smith started as a marketing intern for Tales of the Cocktail in 2014; she is now the events director, with a focus on the Cocktail Apprentice Program (CAP) and the Spirited Awards, deemed the Oscars of the spirits industry. CAP is a mentorship program for bartenders around the world to learn from some of the biggest names in the business. "So many CAPs take what they learned here back to their communities and implement it at their bars, or they teach their friends," says Alex. "We're all learning from each other in different ways, whether that's experiential or emotional." Alex cares deeply about each CAP, keeping in touch with some of them long after the program is over. (Having bartender friends all over the world is a pretty sweet job perk.)

Since 2012, Tales has been honoring extraordinary women in the beverage community at an annual celebration called the Tales Catalyst, formerly known as the Dame Hall of Fame. (You've already met some of them in this book: Misty Kalkofen, Lynnette Marrero, Dr. Joy Spence, Shannon Mustipher, Tiffanie Barriere, and LP O'Brien are all inductees!) In 2023, the Dame Hall of Fame evolved into the Tales Catalyst, with the inclusive name change reflecting that there are other groups who are also fighting for their seat at the table along with women. "There's just something powerful about the spark of a catalyst," Eileen says.

It's pretty astounding that the historically (and currently) male-dominated spirits industry is being transformed by a foundation crafted exclusively by women. Tales of the Cocktail is about being open to new things, learning from those around you, and exploring different interests within the beverage space. But Tales also hosts the hard conversations, like how to make the industry more equitable, sustainable, and diverse, and serves as a platform to help facilitate that change. "It's about building community and sharing ideas," Eileen says. "We bring voices together to help us build what we want for this industry for the future." If Eileen, Lola, and Alex, along with the rest of the Tales team, are the ones leading the way forward for the spirits community everywhere, it's as clear as a cut-crystal glass that we're in good hands.

# CATALYST

In honor of the Tales team, I wanted to create a cocktail that uses only spirits made by women featured in this book. It made sense to turn to a New Orleans classic: the Vieux Carré. First created in the 1930s at the Hotel Monteleone, a Vieux Carré is traditionally made of equal parts rye, brandy, and sweet vermouth, with a touch of Bénédictine and a few dashes of both Angostura and Peychaud's bitters. George Dickel rye (see page 70) is the whiskey of choice here, and Avallen calvados (see page 198) fills the brandy position, giving a lovely apple sweetness. Appleton Estate Signature rum (see page 78) comes to the party and brings that classic Jamaican funk, while Amaro Nonino (see page 188) adds a bittersweet and citrusy note. Of course, there's Angostura bitters and New Orleans–made Peychaud's bitters, plus a touch of rich Demerara syrup, to round out the team. The Catalyst is a cocktail that represents the women who are changing the face of the spirit industry, and in Eileen's words, "This is only the start of where we want to go."

Makes 1 drink

¾ ounce George Dickel rye whiskey

¾ ounce Appleton Estate Signature rum

¾ ounce Avallen calvados

¼ ounce Amaro Nonino

1 barspoon rich Demerara syrup (page 217)

3 dashes Peychaud's bitters

3 dashes Angostura bitters

1 lemon twist, for garnish

Combine the rye, rum, calvados, amaro, Demerara syrup, and both bitters in a rocks glass over one big ice cube and stir until chilled. Garnish with the lemon twist and serve.

RESOURCES & INDEXES

## AGAVE SYRUP
### Makes about 1 cup

½ cup agave nectar

Combine ½ cup hot water and the agave nectar in a nonreactive airtight container. Whisk until combined, then let cool. Cover and store in the refrigerator for up to 3 weeks.

## CINNAMON SYRUP
### Makes about 1½ cups

Handful of cinnamon sticks (about 4)

1 cup Demerara sugar

In a heavy-bottomed medium pot, use a muddler or a wooden spoon to gently crush the cinnamon sticks. Add 1 cup water and bring to a brisk simmer over low heat. Add the sugar and stir until the sugar has fully dissolved. Reduce the heat to maintain a simmer and cook for 30 minutes. Remove from the heat. Fine strain into a nonreactive airtight container and let cool. Cover and store in the refrigerator for up to 3 weeks.

## HIBISCUS SYRUP
### Makes about 1½ cups

1 cup sugar

½ cup dried hibiscus flowers

In a small saucepan, combine 1 cup water and the sugar and bring to a simmer over low heat. Stir until the sugar has fully dissolved. Remove from the heat, then stir in the hibiscus flowers. Let steep for 20 minutes, then fine strain into a nonreactive airtight container and let cool. Cover and store in the refrigerator for up to 2 weeks.

## HONEY SYRUP
### Makes about 1 cup

½ cup honey

Combine ½ cup hot water and the honey in a nonreactive airtight container. Whisk until combined, then let cool. Cover and store in the refrigerator for up to 3 weeks.

## ORGEAT
### Makes 2 cups

1 cup unsweetened almond milk

¾ cup raw cane sugar

¾ cup granulated sugar

2 tablespoons (1 ounce) brandy or cognac, any kind

1½ teaspoons almond extract

½ teaspoon orange blossom water

⅛ teaspoon sea salt

In a medium saucepan, combine the almond milk, cane sugar, and granulated sugar. Heat over medium heat, stirring occasionally, until the sugar has completely dissolved (be careful not to let it boil). Remove from the heat, then stir in the brandy, almond extract, orange blossom water, and salt. Let cool, then transfer to a nonreactive airtight container and cover. Store in the refrigerator for up to 2 months.

## RICH DEMERARA SYRUP
### Makes about 1 cup

1 cup Demerara sugar

In a small saucepan, combine ½ cup water and the sugar and bring to a simmer over low heat. Stir until the sugar has fully dissolved, then remove from the heat and let cool. Transfer to a nonreactive airtight container and cover. Store in the refrigerator for up to 3 weeks.

## SALINE SOLUTION
### Makes ½ cup

1 tablespoon kosher salt

Combine ½ cup hot water and the salt in a nonreactive container and whisk until the salt has fully dissolved. The solution will keep at room temperature indefinitely.

## SIMPLE SYRUP
### Makes about 1½ cups

1 cup sugar

In a small saucepan, combine 1 cup water and the sugar and bring to a simmer over low heat. Stir until the sugar has fully dissolved, then remove from the heat and let cool. Transfer to a nonreactive airtight container and cover. Store in the refrigerator for up to 3 weeks.

## SUPER JUICE (RECIPE BY NICKLE MORRIS)
### Makes about 2¾ cups

4 limes

1½ tablespoons citric acid

1 teaspoon malic acid

Using a Y-shaped peeler, peel the limes and place the peels in a medium nonreactive container; reserve the peeled limes. Add the citric acid and malic acid to the container with the peels and lightly muddle to mix. Let stand for 1 hour to release the oils in the lime peels. Juice the peeled limes and add the lime juice and 2 cups water to the container with the peels. Using an immersion blender, blend until the acids are dissolved and the mixture is fully incorporated (alternatively, transfer the mixture to a standing blender and blend). Fine strain through cheesecloth into a nonreactive airtight container and cover. Store in the refrigerator for up to 2 weeks.

## ACKNOWLEDGMENTS

Thank you to our amazing team at Union Square & Co.: Caitlin Leffel, Lisa Forde, Ivy McFadden, Blanca Oliviery, and everyone else who helped bring this book to life. Thank you to our agent, Jenny Stephens, for always being our tireless champion and cheerleader during the creation of this book and beyond.

*Spirited Women* wouldn't be possible without the spirited women themselves. Thank you to all of our interviewees for sharing your time, your creations, your insights, and of course, your spirits with us. It was a joy to speak with all of you, and we feel so fortunate to be able to share your stories in this way.

Thank you to Peter Browne, John Manolito Cantu, Joanna Carpenter, Laura Del Greco, Lindsay Gardner, Evan Hanczor, Gareth Howells, Rodrigo Lopez, Robby Nelson, Alisha Neverson, Blaire O'Leary, Brad Thomas Parsons, Jake Tennenbaum, Jacob Tschetter, and Gia Vecchio and the team at Foxglove Communications. Huge thank you to the creative souls at The Rockwell Place, especially Alex Kveton and John Carlson, as well as Jorge Bouras and the rest of the folks at Tres Leches. Special thanks to Marie Estrada and Môtô Spirits, and Bianca Miraglia and Uncouth Vermouth.

Finally, thank you to our families and loved ones for all your support and love.
Tom, thank you for reading early drafts and tasting first drafts. I owe you many Montes. (SK)
Love you so, Zach! Sorry again about painting jail! (OM)

## AGAVE

The Ambassador, 205
Burning into the Sea, 133
Chingona, 165
Dream of the Cloud Forest, 121
Kahlo Margarita, 113
Sinergia, 69
Soul of San Miguel, 39
Tree of Life, 93

## AMARO

Le Donne, 193
Queen Bee, 35

## ARAK

Fresh Mist, 187

## AUSTRALIAN WHISKY

Casual Brilliance, 57

## BOURBON WHISKEY

Clara Bow, 105
Femme Fatale, 157
Soda Shoppe, 73
Title IX, 137

## BRANDY

Apples, Apples, Apples, 201
Catalyst, 213
Golden Hour, 173

## CALVADOS

Apples, Apples, Apples, 201

## GIN

A Walk with Jock, 21
Evening Star, 31
Hyde Park Highball, 61
Meemaw's Garden Martini, 77

Obeah Woman, 101
Yellow Brick Road, 89

## LOW ABV

The Ambassador, 205
Best Damn Bellini, 116
Green Light, 153
Le Donne, 193
Punch House Spritz, 125

## IRISH WHISKEY

County Clare Sour, 149

## MASTIHA

The Ambassador, 205

## MEZCAL

Burning into the Sea, 133
Chingona, 165
Dream of the Cloud Forest, 121
Tree of Life, 93

## MOONSHINE

Pretty Little Poison, 143

## NONALCOHOLIC

Berry Smash, 129
Cloaked, 97
Triple Crown, 168

## ÒGÓGÓRÓ

I Am Ours, 179

## PISCO

Golden Hour, 173

## RUM

Catalyst, 213
Globetrotter, 161

Jet-Setter, 183
Joie de Vivre, 83
Mountain Climber, 43
Obeah Woman, 101
Wise Guy, 109

## RYE WHISKEY

Catalyst, 213
Family Tree, 65
Queen Bee, 35
Wise Guy, 109

## SCOTCH WHISKY

Silk Blend, 47

## SHOCHU

Aquariumaid, 52

## SOJU

Green Light, 153

## SOTOL

Un Amor Pendiente, 197

## TENNESSEE WHISKEY

Carry the Torch, 27
Soda Shoppe, 73

## TEQUILA

The Ambassador, 205
Kahlo Margarita, 113
Sinergia, 69
Soul of San Miguel, 39

## VODKA

Evening Star, 31
Old Hag, 209

## WHISKEY

Carry the Torch, 27
Casual Brilliance, 57
Catalyst, 213
Clara Bow, 105
County Clare Sour, 149
Family Tree, 65
Femme Fatale, 157
Queen Bee, 35
Silk Blend, 47
Soda Shoppe, 73
Title IX, 137
Wise Guy, 109

## A

Agave Syrup, 216
The Ambassador, 205
Apple Honey, 201
Apples, Apples, Apples, 201
Aquariumaid, 52
Austin, Nicole, 71–72, 73
A Walk with Jock, 21

## B

Babel, Marva, 99–100, 101
Babel, Myriam, 99–100, 101
Baiocchi, Talia, 123–124, 125
Barnes, Angela, 111–113
Barriere, Tiffanie, 87–88, 89
Berry Smash, 129
Berry Syrup, 129
Best Damn Bellini, 116
Brock, Anne, 59–61
Burning Into the Sea, 133
Butler, Victoria Eady, 23–26, 27

## C

Cardamom Syrup, 43
Carry the Torch, 27
Casual Brilliance, 57
Catalyst, 213
Charred Tomatillo Juice, 197
Cherry Soda Syrup, 73
Chingona, 165
Chitwood, Lauren, 167, 169
Cinnamon Syrup, 216
citrus twist, 15
Clara Bow, 105
Cloaked, 97
Coconut-Washed Mezcal, 93
Cooked Golden Beets, 89
County Clare Sour, 149

## D

Donn's Mix (Babel Edition), 101
Dorda, Alexandra, 181–182, 183
double-straining, 15
dramshops, 84
Dream of the Cloud Forest, 121
Dyer, Carlie, 55–56, 57

## E

Epazote-Infused Cocchi
    Americano, 39
Evening Star, 31

## F

Family Tree, 65
Femme Fatale, 157
Ferguson, Abbey, 167, 169
Freeland Spirits, 75–76
Fresh Mist, 187

## G

Globetrotter, 161
Golden Hour, 173
González Nieves, Bertha, 37–39
Gracie, Lesley, 19–20, 21
Green Light, 153
Grenadine, 105

## H

Hibiscus Syrup, 216
Hibiscus Tea, 129
Hōjicha Tea, 97
Honey Syrup, 216
Hoskin, Karen 41–43
Hyde Park Highball, 61

## I

I Am Ours, 179

## J

Jalapeño-Infused Pueblo Viejo
    Blanco Tequila, 69
Jet-Setter, 183
Jimenez, Yola, 163–165
Joie de Vivre, 83
Jordan, Stephanie, 199–200

## K

Kahlo Margarita, 113
Kalkofen, Misty, 119–121
Kandalaft, Jess, 185–187
Kim, Carolyn, 151–152, 153
Kuehler, Jill, 75–76
Kunkel, Mariah, 91–93

## L

Larsen, Lexie, 167, 169
Lavender-Thyme-Honey
    Syrup, 21
Le Donne, 193

## M

Macleod, Stephanie, 45–46, 47
Marin, Claire, 33–35
Marrero, Lynnette, 103–104, 105
Mary Hebrea, 9
McGuane, Louise, 145–148, 149
McLachlan, Morgan, 29–30,
    31
Meemaw's Garden Martini, 77
Mint Syrup, 169
Miso Syrup, 116
Momosé, Julia, 95–97
Mountain Climber, 43
muddling, 15
Mustipher, Shannon, 107–108,
    109

## N

Nguyen, Jenny, 135–137
Nickle Morris, 133, 218
Nishihira, Selena, 49–52
Nishihira Shuzo, 49–50, 52
Nonino family, 189–192
Nori-Infused Selephant Shochu, 53
Nori-Peppercorn Honey, 133

## O

O'Brien, Lauren Paylor ("LP"),
    127–128, 129
O'Meara, Mallory, 155–156, 157
Obeah Woman, 101
Old Hag, 209
Orange Oleo-Saccharum, 73
Orgeat, 217

## P

Panagopoulos, Effie,
    203–205
Peach Wine, 116
Pedro, Lola, 175–178, 179
Peppermint Tea, 169
Poached Apple Vermouth,
    201
Podoswa Marrun, Nitzan,
    195–196, 197
Pretty Little Poison, 143
Punch House Spritz, 125

## Q

Queen Bee, 35

## R

Ramage, Kelsey, 115–116
Rich Demerara Syrup, 217
Riddle, Renauda, 111–113

**INDEX**

rinsing, 15
rimming a glass, 15
Rodriguez, Rocío, 67–68, 69
Rose Syrup, 193
Rutasikwa, Jacine, 159–160, 161

S

Saline Solution, 217
Scheufele, Romina, 171–173
shaking, 15
dry shaking, 15
Silk Blend, 47
Simple Syrup, 218
Sinergia (large batch variation), 69
Sinergia, 69
Slater, Aubrey, 141–143
Smith, Alex, 212–213
Soda Shoppe, 73
Soul of San Miguel, 39
Spence, Joy, 79–83
Spiced Coffee Syrup, 109
stirring, 15
Sugar Snap Pea–Infused
    Bombay Sapphire Gin, 61
Sumter, Xavier, 113
Super Juice, 133, 218
syrups
        Agave Syrup, 216
        Berry Syrup, 129
        Cardamom Syrup, 43
        Cherry Soda Syrup, 75
        Cinnamon Syrup, 216
        Hibiscus Syrup, 216
        Honey Syrup, 216
        Lavender-Thyme-Honey
            Syrup, 21
        Mint Syrup, 169
        Miso Syrup, 116

Orange Oleo-Saccharum, 75
Orgeat, 217
Rich Demerara Syrup, 217
Rose Syrup, 193
Saline Solution, 217
Simple Syrup, 218
Spiced Coffee Syrup, 109
Tamarind Syrup, 183

T

Tamarind Syrup, 183
Taylor, Bridgette, 207–208
Thomas, Lola, 212–213
Title IX, 137
Tom, Chockie, 131–132, 133
Tree of Life, 93
Triple Crown, 168
Troupe, Molly, 75–76, 77

U

Un Amor Pendiente, 197

V

Villarreal, Carmen, 67–68, 69

W

Wayner, Eileen, 211–213
Wilson, Andrea, 63–65
Wise Guy, 109

Y

Yellow Brick Road, 89